BIMINY
IN DANGER

Andersen Young Readers' Library

For Nigel and Fiona

BIMINY IN DANGER

Brenda Sivers

Illustrated by Jutta Ash

Andersen Press London

First published in 1979 by
Andersen Press Limited
in association with
Hutchinson Limited,
3 Fitzroy Square,
London, W 1

ISBN 0 905478 60 6

Printed in Great Britain

Nicholas flew along the lane, head down, feet pushing the pedals of his bike as fast as he could. As he rounded the corner, he nearly collided with a girl who shrieked with alarm and sprang backwards, narrowly avoiding the speeding wheels.

'Nick! Ouch!'

The girl fell into the hedgerow, grabbing at branches to stop herself from sliding right into the ditch. The wicker basket she had been carrying shot from her arm and a white rabbit, reeling from the shock, sprang out of it and lolloped away.

Nicholas swerved to a halt, nearly doing a somersault over the handlebars.

'Oh, Sarah, for goodness' sake—do you have to moon along in the middle of the road?' he shouted angrily.

'I wasn't in the middle of the road,' the girl retorted, disentangling herself from the hedgerow with difficulty. 'It's you—it's your fault! You ride around like a madman! Look what you've done to my new sweater!' She pulled twigs and burrs from the soft Shetland wool. 'I'll tell M-M-Mummy.'

'I'll tell M-M-Mummy. I'll tell M-M-Mummy,' mimicked her brother in a high, falsetto voice. 'Wait till I'm old enough for a motor bike, then you'll really see me move. I'll come round this corner like greased lightning,' said Nicholas, revving an imaginary engine. 'And before

5

you run and tell Mummy anything, Goody Two Shoes, you'd better pick up that idiotic rabbit of yours—or I'll run him down too.'

And, so saying, the boy jumped on his bike and aimed at the big fluffy rabbit sitting contentedly in the middle of the road.

'Nick! Nick! No, don't!' shrieked Sarah in a panic, running after him. 'Nick, please—' she pleaded as the wheels of her brother's bike threatened to crush it.

But at the very last minute the boy swerved.

'Next time,' he jeered, looking over his shoulder at her and wrinkling his nose like a rabbit. 'Next time I'll get that stupid animal. Squash him flatter than a pancake I will!'

'I'll tell Mu...' Sarah yelled as he raced away, but the words died on her lips. Telling Mother about Nicholas was a waste of time.

'Sarah, love,' her mother would sigh. 'I just don't know what to do about your brother these days. He's— he's....' The woman would raise her hands despairingly. 'He's just impossible since Daddy left.'

'Are you all right, Biminy?' said Sarah, stooping down anxiously by the rabbit. 'Did you get hurt?' And she picked him up and cuddled him in her arms, rocking him back and forth in a soothing way.

'Oh no!' It was Nicholas again. He rounded the corner and shrieked to a halt next to his sister, looking down at her scathingly.

'You and that damned rabbit. It's sickening the way you drool over it.'

Sarah stood up abruptly. 'Don't swear,' she said in a very matter-of-fact tone, and, replacing the rabbit in her basket, she turned her back on her brother and walked away.

'Off to see our little cousins, are we?' he called after her. 'Remember to curtsy first and say please and thank you the way Mummy taught you.' Sarah bit her lip and said nothing. But that only drove her brother to greater excesses.

'Perhaps if you're a very good Goody Two Shoes,' he taunted, riding along beside her, 'Mandy will let you play with all her lovely little dollies and Willy will give you a tune on his violin. Screech! Screech! Screech!' he trilled.

Sarah broke into a run, but the boy kept up.

'And don't let Biminy misbehave,' he said, in a mincing voice. 'Nothing nasty on Uncle Ted's Persian carpets please, or Aunt Angela will scold.'

'Oh shut up!' Sarah snapped.

'Naughty! Naughty! Mummy's nice little girl saying shut up.'

Sarah rounded on him, her face white with rage. 'Look here,' she hissed. 'I've just about had enough from you. I'm getting really f–f–f…, really f–f….' She tried desperately but the wretched words would not come out.

Her brother burst out laughing. 'Poor Goody Two Shoes is getting f–f–f…' he mimicked her stuttering speech until she lashed out at him.

The boy ducked and avoided her flailing fists.

'Sarah is getting really f–f–f…, really f–f–fed up,' he chortled, riding away.

Sarah was mortified. The stammering was new to her but it seemed to happen more and more of late, every time she got angry or nervous. The more she tried to control it, the worse it became. And Nicholas, finding a weak spot in his sister's near-perfect armour, teased her unmercifully. His mother scolded and threatened and

7

pleaded with him, but all in vain. 'Oh N-N-Nicholas, don't be so ridi-di-diculous,' he would chant outside his sister's bedroom, when Mrs Marlowe was out of the house. But Sarah would bury her head in her pillow to muffle the cruel taunts. They used to be good friends, the best of friends, the girl thought sadly as she carried her rabbit along Swallow Lane to her cousins' home.

Nicholas was thirteen, eighteen months older than his sister, but Sarah was big for her age and many people mistook them for twins. Both had dark, wavy hair, deepset brown eyes under straight, rather ferocious eyebrows, snub noses—*retroussé* their mother called them—and determined chins. They were sturdily built and good at anything athletic.

A sunny day found them climbing trees, swimming Badden Lake or riding Farmer Bancroft's ponies.

'Race you to the stream,' Nicholas would cry. And away they'd go, galloping full tilt across the fields, leaping hedges and ditches with yelps of delight.

In winter they went beagling with old Mr Haines or skated on the village pond, if it was really cold.

They were fair students, although the reports they carried home from school usually ended with 'Could do better'. They were popular with the other children in the village and fond of each other, in a teasing kind of way. At least they had been, Sarah sighed, until that awful day just before Christmas when their father had called them into his room and told them that he was leaving.

'Leaving?' Sarah had echoed, her heart taking a nosedive at the terrible word. 'But why?'

Her voice had sounded very faint and distant, as if it belonged to some other person.

'Mummy and I—well, we just don't love each other the way we used to, when we were first married and you

8

and Nicholas came along,' Mr Marlowe said, looking from one to the other, beseeching them to understand. 'So we've decided that, rather than live together unhappily, it would be better for us—and for you—if we lived apart.'

Sarah looked at her father in disbelief. It couldn't be true. It couldn't. Other fathers and mothers split up, she knew that, but her parents were happy together. She was sure of it. They never quarrelled. They never snapped at each other spitefully the way some married people did. There must be another reason, the real reason. Daddy wasn't telling them the truth.

'You don't love us any more,' she said in a whisper, looking into her father's dark, deepset eyes.

'Waggles'—her father used his pet name for her— 'you know that isn't true. I love you and Nick more than anything and anyone in the whole wide world but....' He raised his hands in a gesture of helplessness. 'I just can't stay in this house. You know what it's like when you fall out with someone who's been a close friend. You don't even have to fall out with them, you just— well, you just grow apart—and become different people going in different directions. You have nothing in common with them any more—and it's like that with Mummy and me. We simply....'

'But you do love Mummy, you do!' interrupted Sarah, willing it to be true. 'You *are* happy together,' she insisted, refusing to face the bleak prospect of her parents' separation.

Mr Marlowe only shook his head. 'We've tried to put a good face on it—for your sake,' he said. 'Mummy and I have known for a long time that our marriage was in trouble. Believe me, darling, we've done everything we could....'

9

But Sarah wasn't listening. The tears poured down her cheeks and she flung herself at her father, imploring him to stay.

'Daddy, don't go! Please don't go!' she begged him. 'Nick...!' She reached out to her brother, urging him to add his pleas to her own. But Nicholas said nothing. He sat all the while with his head bent, his mouth tightly shut, staring unblinkingly at the pattern on the carpet as if he were mesmerized by it.

'Nick!' Sarah cried to him. But he ignored her.

'Nick, old man'—his father reached out to him, touching his face—'I'll be going away for a time, to the Middle East. My company's opening a big plant in Abu Dhabi and I'm going to work on the plans. I'm sorry it's happened at a time like this but, in a way, it's a good thing. It will give me time to—well, sort myself out a bit. When I come back, I'm going to take a flat in Cheltenham. That's only a few miles away, isn't it, so we'll be seeing each other often, as often as you like. O.K., old fellow?'

Nicholas nodded but he didn't look up. And he moved his head away from his father's touch.

That was eight months ago, Sarah thought, eight bleak months and still their father hadn't returned. There had been letters from him at the beginning, lots of them, telling them about his life in the Middle East and how exciting it was to work there. He said how much he missed them, how he was longing to see them again—but then a new note began to creep in. He apologized repeatedly for not returning—too much work, he said, too much to do—maybe in a few months he'd get back, maybe a little longer....

After a while the letters got fewer—and briefer. They were written hastily and they said very little.

'Do you think he's going to stay there for ever? Do you think we'll ever see him again?' Sarah asked her brother anxiously as the months passed. 'Do you think he's forgotten us?'

But Nicholas said nothing. He simply refused to talk about it—to anyone.

'Hello, sweetheart, what's up?'

Sarah jumped. She had been so deep in thought, so lost in memories of her father, she hadn't even noticed the man walking towards her along Swallow Lane.

'Oh, Uncle Ted, it's n-n-nothing,' she stammered.

'Something upset you?' The man knelt down and looked at the girl's tear-stained face. 'What happened?'

Sarah only shook her head and stared at the pavement.

'Well, how's Biminy then?' he smiled, peering at the Angora rabbit in Sarah's basket.

'He's a b-b-bit shaken up too,' Sarah said. 'He's just had a nasty accident,' she added, and instantly regretted it.

Her uncle waited expectantly for details but the girl stayed silent, hoping he wouldn't press her. Nicholas was becoming more unbearable with every passing day but she wouldn't tell tales about him.

'Well.' Her uncle straightened up. 'You both look a bit shaken up to me,' he said. 'So I suggest you come home and we'll see what we can find to put a smile back on your face. A lettuce leaf for Biminy, I suppose, and I happen to know that cook has made a big batch of scones this morning. So if you and I could find a pot of strawberry jam and a dish of whipped cream, we'd be in business, wouldn't we?' And he winked at her in a mischievous way.

Sarah smiled and took his outstretched hand. She was really too old to walk hand in hand with her uncle, she thought, but there was nobody in sight and, besides, it was such a big, comforting hand she could hardly resist it.

They went along Swallow Lane chatting casually, Sarah trying to keep up with the man's long, loping gait. He was tall, well over six foot, and a champion sprinter in his younger days. Not at all like her father, she thought. Mr Marlowe was short and thickset and cricket had been his game.

'What a marvellous day,' said her uncle, tilting back his head so that the hot sun shone full on his face. 'I hope this good weather holds till Saturday. Amanda will shoot herself it if rains.'

Saturday was Amanda's ninth birthday and the cause of considerable commotion over the past weeks. Since the little girl had lived in the village for such a short time, she hardly knew any other children, except her cousins. So she had been allowed to invite some of her friends from her old home in Birmingham.

'I thought you were going to put a marquee in the garden,' said Sarah, who had heard the plans for the party a hundred times over from her excited cousin.

'Oh, we are—but it won't be much fun if we all have to squelch back and forth from the house, will it?'

'Is it a big marquee?' The only other one Sarah had ever seen was at the village fête, and that had been huge.

'It's big enough to hold forty or fifty people.'

'Forty or fifty people!' Sarah was impressed. She had never had more than six friends to her birthday parties. But then, she thought ruefully, her home wasn't big enough to hold more, whereas Amanda's was big enough to hold an army.

'Well, they're not all Amanda's friends,' admitted Uncle Ted. 'Aunt Angela and I thought we'd make it a kind of double event, you know, a house warming as well as a birthday party for Amanda. So we've invited some of our own friends—as well as aunts and uncles and assorted cousins,' he laughed.

Sarah made a face.

'What does Amanda think of that?' she said, knowing full well what she would think if her mother foisted a lot of fuddy duddy grown-ups on her birthday party.

'She's a bit put out,' agreed Uncle Ted, 'and maybe it was rather mean of us,' he conceded. 'But, anyway....' He shrugged it off.

They walked in silence until they reached a great iron gate with the letter 'G' wrought into the middle of it. 'Here we are,' said Uncle Ted, holding the gate open for Sarah.

The 'G' stood for 'The Grange', an impressive Elizabethan half-timbered mansion, the biggest house in Croxley and for centuries the ancestral home of the Hamilton de Veres, an aristocratic family directly descended, so they said, from Charles the Second. Despite their illustrious background, however, the Hamilton de Veres had fallen on hard times, like many other landed gentry, and they had sold The Grange to Sarah's uncle, a wealthy businessman.

A long, gravel path led past carefully tended lawns and flower beds to the big black and white house that stood secluded and sheltered by towering elms and pine trees. As Sarah and her uncle drew near, three great black labradors came bounding round the side of the house barking excitedly.

Sarah shrank away from them. She wasn't afraid of the dogs, but the rabbit in her basket stirred uneasily at the sound of the barking and she wanted to protect him from any further upsets.

'I'll put the mutts away,' said her uncle, 'then you and I will slip into the kitchen, outwit the indomitable Mrs Kennan and help ourselves to an outrageous number of scones. O.K?'

Sarah laughed. Uncle Ted was always joking, always in good spirits.

The indomitable Mrs Kennan, the resident cook at The Grange, was not to be outwitted, however.

'They're not cool enough to eat yet, Mr Allen,' she said sternly, standing protectively in front of the scones. 'Besides, they'll give you a bad attack of indigestion,' she added, cutting short any possible protests. She had been the Hamilton de Veres' cook, inherited by Sarah's uncle, and she wasn't going to let anyone tell her what to do in her own kitchen.

'There's gingerbread,' she conceded, after a moment's thought, 'or chocolate cake with butter icing, if you'd prefer it.'

Uncle Ted looked at Sarah.

'Chocolate cake, please.'

'Chocolate cake for the lady, Mrs Kennan,' he said breezily, 'a succulent lettuce leaf for the lady's handsome rabbit and a cup of tea for me, please. We'll be in the conservatory.'

'Very well, sir. The children are already there.'

'And Mrs Allen?'

'She's gone into Cheltenham, sir, to visit her sister. She said to tell you she'll be back around six o'clock and please not to forget that the Arnotts are coming to dinner.'

'Oh hell, yes.' Mr Allen made a face. 'I had completely forgotten. And I was hoping to have a quiet evening for a change. Oh well....' He shrugged. 'Come on, Sarah, let's go and find the kids—they're probably stuffing themselves with cake at the moment.' He led the way into the sunny conservatory at the back of the great house.

William was curled up in an armchair, a piece of cake in one hand, a book in the other. Sarah sometimes wondered if her cousin went anywhere without something to read—and he never bothered with schoolboy adventures either. William's idea of a first-rate book was *The History of the Celtic Races* or *A Thinking Man's Guide to Chess*.

He looked up when his father and cousin came into the room and peered at them through his thick glasses.

'Good cake,' he said to Sarah, demolishing the last mouthful. 'You should have some.'

'I'd like to—if there's any left.'

'I thought you were having a music lesson about now?' said Mr Allen.

The boy shook his head. 'Prof. Hackett couldn't make it. He phoned about half an hour ago. He wants to know if I can go over to his house tomorrow morning. Apparently there's a brilliant violinist coming over from Germany and he'd like me to meet him. Will you drive me over, Dad?'

The boy's eyes shone; the thought of spending a few hours with a fellow musician was more thrilling to him than flying to the moon in a spaceship or winning the

15

Grand Prix. But his father didn't look so delighted.

'Professor Hackett certainly knows how to spoil a man's day of rest,' he sighed. 'Perhaps Mum will take you. She and Amanda can visit Grandma at the same time. By the way, where is Amanda? Mrs Kennan said she was with you.'

The boy shrugged. 'Don't know,' he said innocently, but he winked at Sarah.

'Well, I...' began Mr Allen, looking round the room, and then he caught sight of a plate on the table with a half-eaten slice of cake on it and he smiled. 'Well, I'm sorry she's not here,' he said, raising his voice, 'because I have something very special for her.'

There was a scuffling sound behind the curtain and a girl suddenly appeared, her eyes bright with excitement.

'What? What have you got for me?' she cried, hurling herself at her father.

'Me!' he said, picking her up and twirling her round his head as if she were a baby.

'Oh, Daddy, you are rotten!' cried the girl, hugging him delightedly.

Sarah looked away. It was too painful a reminder of her own relationship with her father. But her uncle, catching sight of her face, reached out and drew her into the group, putting an arm affectionately around her waist.

'Sarah!' Amanda grabbed her cousin by the shoulder. 'Come with me,' she said, pulling the girl after her. 'I want to show you my party dress—it's just arrived. Oh, may we, Daddy?' she added, although she was halfway out of the door.

He nodded. 'But don't give Sarah a hard time,' he cautioned his daughter. 'She's a bit upset.'

'Are you, Sarah?' said Amanda, as the two of them

16

raced upstairs to the bedrooms. 'What's wrong?'

'Oh nothing.' Sarah shrugged it off, wishing her uncle hadn't mentioned it. It made her feel different, as if she were someone special, only in the wrong kind of way. But her cousin wasn't interested anyway. She had her mind on something far more enthralling.

'Here's my dress,' she said, bursting into her room and pointing to the bed. 'Isn't it pretty? Mrs Hazeldeane made it for me—yes, well, that isn't what I really wanted to show you,' she said, pulling a confused Sarah away from the bed and whispering into her ear. 'I know what I'm getting for my birthday.'

'What?'

'Ssh!' Amanda put a finger to her lips and motioned her cousin to follow her. At the bedroom door she stopped and looked to the left and right, checking that nobody was around.

Sarah giggled. 'You look like something out of a silly film....'

But Amanda rounded on her angrily. 'Be quiet!' she snapped. 'If anyone hears us, I'll be in trouble. Come on!' And she tiptoed quickly down the long corridor.

Sarah followed, wondering what the birthday present might be. Something fabulous, no doubt. It always was. In years past, Sarah and Nicholas had always gone to the Allens' home in Birmingham for the various birthday and Christmas parties. And always the gifts for them and their cousins had been lavishly expensive. 'More than we can afford,' grumbled Sarah's mother every time, 'but then I don't believe in wasting a lot of money on toys.'

'Sour grapes!' laughed her husband. 'I'd love to have a lot of money to waste on anything.'

'This is my mother's work room,' whispered Amanda,

18

stopping in front of a door at the very end of the corridor. 'She does painting and stuff in here. Come on!' And, pulling Sarah into the room, she closed the door quietly behind them.

'Where is it then?' Sarah looked round but couldn't see anything that might be her cousin's birthday present.

There was a huge easel by the window and a table covered with oil paints and brushes and pieces of dirty rag. Paintings in various stages of progress were propped against the walls, but Sarah couldn't imagine that one of them was for Amanda's birthday. They were all strangely abstract subjects, lines and circles and things.

'It's over there.' Amanda pointed to a table in one corner covered with what appeared to be a pile of dust covers, the kind used to protect furniture when people moved house.

Sarah was puzzled until Amanda pulled away the covers with a flourish—and then she let out a gasp of surprise.

'A dolls' house,' she breathed. 'Oh, it's so beautiful. I've always wanted a ....' But she checked herself in mid-sentence. It was a point of honour with her never to covet any of her cousin's toys, however much she longed for them. Amanda laughed out loud at her cousin's face, then quickly slapped a hand over her mouth.

'It is lovely, isn't it?' she whispered. 'I discovered it quite by accident the other day. Mummy asked me to fetch something from her room and I couldn't find it, as usual,' she added, pulling a face, 'so I started searching around—and that's how I found the house. Isn't it lovely?' she said again, hugging herself with delight. 'You

19

won't tell them I know about it, will you? Promise?'
Sarah shook her head. She put Biminy's basket on the
floor and knelt down in front of the house.

'I'll open it up for you.'

Amanda put her finger to a spring at the side of the
dolls' house and the front wall sprang open, revealing
the inner rooms.

'Why it's—it's....' Sarah was too surprised to speak.

'It's our house,' laughed Amanda, but silently this
time. 'It's an exact copy of The Grange, isn't it? But
don't touch anything, please. They'd kill me if they knew
I'd seen it.'

Sarah was in seventh heaven. The dolls' house was
perfect in every detail—the rooms, the furniture, even
tiny clocks and mirrors. It was The Grange in miniature.

'You can come and play with it whenever you want,'
said Amanda.

'Oh I will! I will!'

Sarah loved The Grange. She always had. As a little
girl she had stood for hours, her forehead pressed
against the cold iron of the gates, gazing in wonder at
the fairy people, the magical people who lived in such a
palace. The Hamilton de Veres had a butler and maids
and gardeners and under gardeners. They swept in and
out of the great gates in a chauffeur-driven Daimler,
smiling at Sarah and waving like royalty as they went by.
Their daughters rode piebald ponies, trotting round the
grounds in their riding habits and velvet caps. In winter
the girls wore red coats trimmed with fur and rode
around in a shiny black trap pulled by a little Shetland
pony. Sometimes they came to the gate and spoke to
Sarah, but they never invited her in. An enchanted
world, it seemed to the girl, a dream world. So different
from her life in the little cottage near Croxley Cross-

roads.

Then one day, as she was wandering home from school, kicking stones and thinking listlessly about the pile of homework Mrs Prince had given her, Sarah saw a large white board outside the gates of The Grange. As she drew level with it, her heart missed a beat.

'For Sale,' it announced in bold black letters. 'Sole Agents: Messrs Mincham & Mincham, High Street, Cheltenham.'

Sarah rushed home, beside herself with excitement.

'Buy it? Us—buy The Grange?' her father had echoed in amazement. 'We couldn't even afford one wing!'

And he had burst out laughing at the very idea.

Sarah was bitterly disappointed. She pleaded and wept until her mother brought her up short.

'Of course you'd like to live in The Grange,' she snapped. 'I would too. And I'd like to drive around in a chauffeured car and have maids to do the housework and buy a yacht and spend every winter in the south of France, but I can't because we can't afford it. We have a nice home here. It isn't big, but it's better than many people have, and I've learned to be content with what I have. You'll have to learn that lesson too, my girl.'

So Sarah learned her lesson—or pretended to. But in her heart she secretly resolved that when she grew up, she would buy The Grange and live there herself with ponies and dogs and cats and guinea pigs and—oh, it would be a marvellous life. She could hardly wait for it to begin.

The Hamilton de Veres moved out one cold, dreary day in November. Sarah watched rather sadly as the big moving vans lumbered down the gravel path and out into Swallow Lane. The Daimler came last, with the family huddled together in the back.

21

'Goodbye, my dear,' said Mrs Hamilton de Vere, rolling down the window and extending a gloved hand to Sarah. 'Take care of yourself,' she added, her voice heavy with sadness. An aroma of perfume and face powder, and vaguely of moth balls too, floated out of the elegant interior of the Daimler and engulfed Sarah.

'Goodbye,' said the girl. She wanted to ask if anyone had bought The Grange yet, because she was dying to know, but there was always something rather forbidding about Mrs Hamilton de Vere, and Sarah had the feeling it was a 'personal' question, as her mother would say, like asking adults how old they were, though Sarah could never understand what was so wrong about that. So she stayed silent and waved the Hamilton de Veres out of The Grange and out of her life.

The 'For Sale' sign stayed up for more than a year. The house stood empty and silent; the great mullioned windows, which had twinkled with warm lights on dark winter evenings, were black and mournful now. The rooms which had glittered to the sparkle of crystal chandeliers were gloomy, dust gathering on the mantelpieces, spiders weaving webs in the corners of the ceiling.

'They'll never get rid of that white elephant,' said Mr Marlowe. 'Must cost an arm and a leg to run a place like that.'

'How much would it cost—to buy it, I mean?' said Sarah.

'Why?' her father laughed. 'Were you planning to?'

Sarah blushed. She hated it when people made fun of her and, though she knew it was silly, she did wonder from time to time how long it would take her to get together enough money to buy The Grange.

'I was just asking, that's all,' she mumbled, looking

embarrassed.

'Sorry, Waggles,' Mr Marlowe apologized. 'I'm not sure but I think they want about seventy-five or eighty thousand for it.'

'Pounds?' Sarah echoed in amazement.

'That's right,' said her father, trying not to laugh because he didn't want his daughter to think he was making fun of her again.

Sarah thought about it for a while. Eighty thousand pounds was more money than she could make in ten lifetimes, wasn't it?

'And how much did our house cost?' she asked.

'Oh, it was six thousand when we bought it in 1971, so I imagine it's worth well'—her father did some rapid calculations in his head—'about twenty-three or twenty-four thousand today.'

'Oh.'

He smiled. 'Yes, there's quite a difference between our little shed and The Grange, isn't there, Waggles?' He tweaked her nose playfully. 'But then I'm only a poor architect, so this is all I can afford.'

Sarah's father often referred to himself disparagingly as 'only a poor architect' but Sarah knew he was a very good one. Everybody said so. But obviously, she thought ruefully, even good architects didn't make enough money to buy big houses like The Grange.

'What will happen if nobody buys it?' Sarah wondered out loud. 'Will they bring the price down, do you think?'

'They might,' said Mr Marlowe, 'although I don't think they'll ever bring it down to something you can afford, sweetheart. Not yet, anyway,' he added, trying to keep his face as straight as possible. 'On the other hand, they might sell it at the asking price and split it up into flats, the way they did with The Manor in Verton.'

'Oh no!' Sarah was horrified. The Grange couldn't become a block of flats. It was unthinkable.

'I know. I don't like the idea either,' agreed her father, 'but I'm afraid it's on the cards, unless they find a very rich man to buy it. And I'd say that's not very likely. Croxley's a bit of a backwater, you know. Nothing much to attract the jet set around here.'

Sarah was downcast. It began to look as if The Grange would never belong to her after all. The beautiful dream was fading fast—the horses and dogs and cats and guinea pigs with it. But shortly afterwards something happened that put The Grange and its financial problems right out of her mind.

Her father left home.

For a while, after Mr Marlowe had quietly packed all his clothes and books and left, the little house at Croxley Crossroads went into mourning.

Nicholas was sullen and silent. He answered his mother and sister in brief, terse sentences and never mentioned his father, not even when letters started arriving from Abu Dhabi. Most of the time he stayed in his room, behind a locked door, or he rode round the country lanes on his bike—alone.

Sarah had bad dreams and many nights she woke screaming and clutching at the sheet in a frenzy of fear. Mrs Marlowe would comfort her, cradling her in her arms, murmuring words of consolation.

'Is it something I did, Mummy?' the girl would cry, choked by racking sobs. 'Did Daddy hate me?'

Over and over again her mother tried to reassure her. 'It wasn't your fault, darling. It wasn't. It's something between Daddy and me. When you're older, you'll understand. It isn't easy for two people to get along well and marriage is such a close relationship. If it isn't right,

24

if it isn't working well, it's better for the couple to go their separate ways. Otherwise they'll start to get—well, spiteful with each other. And that's horrible—for everyone.'

Sarah nodded agreement but she sensed that her mother wasn't happy either. She was bright and cheerful, in a determined kind of way, but often she would snap at her children or erupt into bouts of temper for the flimsiest of reasons.

Sarah would have liked to confide in Nicholas, the way they used to, sitting on each other's beds at night, swapping secrets, giggling—but he rejected her now, lashing out angrily whenever she tried to get close to him.

Inquisitive friends at school asked her questions, hurtful, probing questions about her father that made her feel they despised her. And the children in the village looked at her strangely, or so she thought, as if they pitied her.

Gradually she withdrew from them all. Outwardly she was still the same friendly, pleasant girl she had always been, but she never stayed for games after school any more, stopped inviting friends to her home and always found a convenient excuse for not going to theirs.

She spent most of her time caring for Biminy, clearing out his hutch, grooming him and scouring the countryside for wild plants and herbs—plantain, dandelion, shepherd's purse, hedge parsley, coltsfoot, knapweed, sow thistle and many more—to satisfy his voracious appetite.

One cold, wintry afternoon as Sarah walked home from school, she saw a big car outside her house, a maroon car with a silver leopard on its bonnet. Intrigued, she peered inside. None of her mother's friends had such a large, obviously expensive car. And then she suddenly realized who it belonged to and bursting into the house, she cried out, 'Uncle Ted! Uncle Ted!'

The living room door opened abruptly and a man came out, arms outstretched, a big welcoming grin on his face.

'Hi, sweetheart,' he said, hugging her as hard as he could. 'Good to see you.'

Uncle Ted was her mother's only brother, a tall, gangling kind of man with curly blond hair and a shaggy moustache that tickled when Sarah kissed him. He lived with his wife and two children in a huge flat that took up the top two floors of an apartment block in Edgbaston, a wealthy suburb of Birmingham. Sarah wasn't sure what her uncle did for a living but Mr Marlowe always referred to him as a 'tycoon' and sometimes a 'plutocrat'.

'What is a plu— plutocrat?' Sarah asked.

'Something I'd like to be but never will,' her father laughed.

'What is a plutocrat?' she asked her teacher. And Mrs Prince laughed too.

'A plutocrat is a very wealthy, powerful man. Why do you ask, Sarah?' she said. 'Do you know one?'

Sarah smiled shyly, wondering if it was right to tell her teacher about Uncle Ted.

'I think—er—one of my relatives is one,' she said. 'Oh—how nice.'

Was Mrs Prince making fun of her, she wondered?

'And what is this relative's name? Perhaps we all know him too?'

The other children in the class started giggling but Mrs Prince silenced them with a look.

Sarah was beginning to feel thoroughly embarrassed and wished she hadn't brought up the wretched subject.

'His name's Ted—I mean Edward, Edward Allen. And he lives in Birmingham. I think he has factories there too.'

'Edward Allen!' Mrs Prince looked impressed. 'My goodness, if it's the Edward Allen I'm thinking of, he's one of the biggest manufacturers of plastics in the whole country.'

Sarah looked at the man sitting in front of her at that very moment. An ordinary man, she thought, nothing special to look at—just nice old Uncle Ted who always called her his favourite niece and brought her marvellous presents.

'Uncle Ted has some very exciting news for you,' said her mother, coming into the room with a tray of sandwiches and cakes. 'You tell her, Ted,' she said, looking at her brother.

He reached out and drew Sarah towards him.

'Aunt Angela and I are getting pretty fed up with living in a big city all the time,' he said. 'We'd like to move to the country, to a nice quiet little village like this one. And we think it will be good for Amanda and William too.'

Sarah felt her heart start to thump a little harder. She knew what he would say next—at least, she prayed he would say it.

'Since—since your father isn't here any more'—he seemed ill at ease when he said that, Sarah noticed—'we'd like to live close to you and Nicholas and your mother, so....'

Sarah held her breath. Please God, she thought, make him say it. Make him say it!

'So we've bought The Grange.'

'I knew it! I knew it!' The girl let out a shout of delight and, breaking away from her uncle, she did a little

27

wardance around the room.

'The Grange! The Grange!' she whooped. 'I'll be able to go there often, won't I, to see you and Aunt Angela? I won't be a nuisance.'

'Sweetheart,' said her uncle, kissing her, 'I'll be very annoyed if you don't come and see us at least ten times a day.'

Sarah was beside herself with excitement. The great house was not to be hers, not yet, anyway, but at least it would be in her family. She could actually walk through those big iron gates, along the wide, gravelled path to the double oak doors and then—and then she would actually be inside.

The 'For Sale' sign came down and an army of plasterers, painters, carpenters and cleaners moved in. Every afternoon, on her way home from school, Sarah checked their progress, asking questions, making comments, complimenting, criticizing, as if the house were her own.

'Done to your satisfaction, is it, madam?' the workmen would say, smiling down at her from the top of their long ladders as they painted ceilings or repaired woodwork. And Sarah would nod approval.

Everything about The Grange was to her satisfaction. It was just as she had imagined it would be: a great entrance hall with a magnificent flight of stairs up to the first landing, oak-panelled rooms, open fireplaces—big enough to sit in, some of them—a beautiful conservatory overlooking the garden, kennels, stables—oh, it was a palace. And Sarah wandered through it spellbound.

A month or so later, Uncle Ted and his family moved in. And Sarah was their very first visitor.

'I've brought you these,' she said, offering her aunt a

bouquet of wild flowers she had picked that afternoon from Farmer Bancroft's meadow. 'They're a house-warming present.'

'How kind of you, darling.' Aunt Angela took the flowers but then she frowned. 'Somewhere in all those wretched boxes....' She pointed to the crates that seemed to cover almost every inch of floor space. 'Somewhere in all that mess is a vase for these pretty flowers. But where?' She shook her head in despair.

'I'll go now.' Sarah backed away. Her aunt seemed tired and disgruntled by the move. Her long blonde hair, usually piled high on her head in a glossy chignon, now resembled a bird's nest. Pieces kept coming adrift and falling into the woman's eyes, much to her annoyance. Her nail polish was chipped and there was the beginning of a ladder in her stocking. She was not the elegant woman Sarah was used to seeing.

'Perhaps those men could find the vase for you,' she suggested, indicating a group of men in the hall who were busily unpacking boxes and shouting, 'Where does this table go?' and 'What shall we do with this book case?'

'Oh, no use asking them!' snapped her aunt irritably. 'Professional packers. Huh!' she fumed. 'It would have been simpler if I'd done the packing myself! And where on earth is Ted?'

'I'll go now.' Sarah backed away. Anger frightened her and Aunt Angela did seem very put out by the move.

'Somewhere here. It must be somewhere here,' her aunt mumbled, walking among the boxes and swearing under her breath as she caught her stockings yet again. 'It's got to be here....'

'I'll go now.' Sarah edged towards the door. ''Bye.'

'What?' Aunt Angela looked up sharply. 'Oh darling,

sorry.' She came towards Sarah and took her hand. 'I'm in such an awful mood, aren't I? Forgive me. Stay and have tea with us. We've got plates and cups, I'm sure I'll find them soon.' She managed to laugh. 'And Amanda's gone to the village shop to get cakes and things. And Sarah, love,' she added, looking earnestly into the girl's face, 'come whenever you like, all right? No invitations. You and your brother are always welcome, you know that.'

But Sarah needed no persuading. The Grange was a beautiful dream, and she was living in it. The Grange was warm and welcoming, somewhere she could run to when Nicholas was too horrible to bear or her mother's tense moods oppressed her. At The Grange she could forget her troubles, for a while at least. Amanda and William never spoke about her father, never even mentioned the separation and impending divorce. In fact, they pretended that life was going on as it always had, a pretence Sarah enjoyed while she was with them.

They were not the kind of friends she was used to. Amanda was a delicate little girl, almost frail. She loved making clothes for her dolls, or painting with her mother or squashing wild flowers between the pages of a scrapbook, while William was studious—a clever scholar and a talented musician. Sarah was too impatient for books, too active for sewing or sketching. She was a country girl, through and through, a swim-across-the-pond-beat-you-to-the-end-of-the-field girl. But she found a quiet comfort in her cousins, a comfort she needed so badly.

'Where've you been—as if I didn't know?' sneered Nicholas when Sarah got home later that afternoon. 'Playing with Mandy Pandy and silly Willy,' he trilled in a girlish voice before she could answer.

'And what's wrong with that?'

'I don't know how you can spend all your time with them—they're a couple of creeps.'

Nicholas was lying on the chesterfield in the living room, a pile of records on the floor next to him, rock music blaring from the record player so loudly the whole house seemed to vibrate to the raucous sound. From the look of the mess around him—dirty plates and glasses, sweet wrappers, apple cores—he had been there all day.

'What did you do—play dollies with Mandy Pandy?' he jeered. 'Or was it doctors and nurses today?'

Sarah stiffened. She usually tried to ignore her brother's taunts, but his sneering contempt of their cousins was too much for her. Besides, she hadn't played doctors and nurses for years.

'We talked about her birthday party on Saturday,' she said, with as much dignity as she could muster. 'They're going to have a marquee on the back lawn and a juggler and a....'

'And Namby Pamby will wear a taffeta dress with white daisies all over it and little satin shoes with pom poms.'

'Oh, really!' Sarah turned away in disgust. It was impossible to talk sensibly with her brother any more.

'And what about wee Willy?' Nicholas said, warming to the attack. He knew when he was getting under his sister's skin and it seemed to delight him. 'I'll bet you had to listen to him torturing his violin. "Oh, do listen to dear little William play. He's so gifted, so gifted,"' Nicholas imitated Aunt Angela's rather high-pitched voice.

'And so he is,' Sarah retorted hotly. 'He's very clever....'

'I know, I know.' Nicholas sprang to his feet in an agitated kind of way. 'Cousin Willy is the eighth wonder of the world. He gets up at the crack of dawn, lisps his prayers, kisses Mummy and Daddy good morning, reads ten pages of Latin, embroiders doilies for....'

'Oh shut up!' Sarah cut him short. 'You're just jealous.'

'Jealous?' Her brother exploded. 'Jealous of that little...?'

'Just because you can't do the things he can, you spend all your time jeering at him. I think you're secretly jealous of William and Amanda because they have so much—that's why you never go to The Grange.'

'I never go the Grange because the place stinks.' Nicholas was full of disdain. 'And I wouldn't give you that'—he snapped his fingers—'for anything they have!' Throwing himself down on the chesterfield again, he reached under a cushion and drew out a packet of cigarettes.

Sarah's face darkened. 'M–Mummy said....'

'M–Mummy said. M–Mummy said,' mimicked her brother.

'You know you're not allowed to smoke.' Sarah watched in horror as the boy struck a match and put it to the end of the cigarette. 'When Mummy comes home she'll smell the smoke and she'll be furious. Why do you

33

keep making her angry? Oh N–N–Nicholas....'

Her brother leaped to his feet, puffing smoke into the girl's face. 'Oh N–N–Nicholas, don't be so ridi–di–dicu-lous!' he sang, gloating in his sister's discomfort.

Sarah turned on her heel and ran upstairs, Nicholas in hot pursuit, shouting the cruel refrain at the top of his voice.

'I'm going to puff smoke through the keyhole,' he yelled as she locked her bedroom door. 'Then Mum will think it's you who's been smoking and you'll be for it instead of me, little Miss Goody Two Shoes.'

'Go away!'

'I'm puffing smoke through now. Here it comes. Can you smell it? Can you…?'

The front door suddenly slammed and their mother's voice barked, 'Nicholas! Come down here! At once!'

Sarah heard him shuffle down the stairs, then she clapped her hands over her ears. She didn't want to hear another of those horrible fights between her mother and Nicholas. They happened so often of late, too often. And after the fight there would be such tension in the house, Nicholas sulky, her mother abrupt and ill-tem-pered.

She took Biminy out of his basket and placed him gently on the floor. There would be all hell to pay too if her mother knew she had the rabbit in her room—that was absolutely forbidden—but Biminy was something special, much more than a pet. Biminy was warm and soft and gentle. Without him, the little house at Croxley Crossroads would have been unbearable for Sarah.

The rabbit sat for a while, bemused, then decided it was high time he had a wash and brush up. Balancing on his hind legs, he licked the pads of his forepaws, coating them with saliva, and pressed them close together over

34

the side of his face in rapid, brushing movements. When he was quite certain that his face was squeaky clean, he washed his ears in the same way. Then he licked both sides of his body and the fur beneath his feet. He appeared to be totally absorbed in his toilet, oblivious to the outside world, but at the slightest movement from Sarah he froze, a startled, intent expression on his pretty little face.

'Dear old Biminy,' said the girl, stroking him gently, 'you're such a beautiful boy.'

And he was. Biminy was an Angora, an aristocrat among rabbits. His long, silky white fur stood out like a halo round his fat little body. After he had licked his coat thoroughly, Sarah always ran a brush through the fur, to remove any tangles. She had inherited the rabbit just after her father left for the Middle East.

'Elizabeth's had her babies,' Mrs Marlowe had said one day when Sarah got home from school. 'They were born this morning.'

'Oh, Mummy, may I go and see them now?'

Mrs Marlowe nodded. 'But don't be late for di...' she began, but Sarah was already halfway up the road to Mrs Oliver's house, running like the wind.

'May I see them?' she said breathlessly to the stout, grey-haired woman who opened the door to her.

Mrs Oliver smiled and stood aside. 'Of course you may, m'dear. You know the way,' she said, and Sarah sped past her, through the house, pausing only to say a hasty 'Hello' to Mr Oliver, who was sitting at the kitchen table reading the evening paper, and out into the garden. The rabbits were kept in a white-washed out-house just past the lettuce patch.

There was a big hutch in one corner with a fluffy white rabbit sitting contentedly in the hay, dozing fitfully. But its eyes snapped open as Sarah burst into the shed and ran up to the hutch.

'We're so pleased,' said Mrs Oliver, who had followed the girl at a more leisurely pace. 'Eight kittens she's had. Eight! Imagine that! You're a clever girl, Elizabeth, yes you are,' she said affectionately to the rabbit which gazed back at her impassively.

'I can't see them at all,' said Sarah, peering through the wire netting at the front of the hutch. 'There's still that great pile of fur in one corner but I can't see anything in it.'

'Come here then.' Mrs Oliver took her elbow. 'We've cut a hole in the top, right over the nest, so we can keep an eye on the kittens without Elizabeth knowing.'

Sarah stood on tiptoe and peered into the hutch. 'Oh,' she exclaimed. 'Oh, they're sweet.'

Eight tiny bodies lay curled up in a pile of their mother's soft fur. Eight blind, deaf, naked little creatures huddled together for warmth and comfort.

'May I hold one?' she said hopefully.

But the woman shook her head. 'Rabbit mothers are very touchy about people handling their young,' she explained. 'They'll kill their kittens at the slightest provocation.'

Sarah was aghast. No mother could be so cruel. 'It can't be true!' she exclaimed. But Mrs Oliver was adamant.

'Oh yes, it is,' she assured her. 'You wait till they're a little older and Elizabeth isn't feeling so possessive about them. Then you can take them out and play with them all you like.'

Sarah looked at Elizabeth doubtfully. She couldn't believe the dear old rabbit would kill her own kittens. It had to be an old wives' tale, some silly story Mrs Oliver had picked up from the country folk.

The Olivers had run the village shop for years, working tirelessly day in, year out, until it had all got too much for the old couple and they had retired gratefully to the peace of their little cottage by Croxley Green.

'It's good to rest at last,' Mr Oliver had said, leaning back in his armchair, but before many months had passed he had bought a patch of land near his home and started to grow vegetables which he sold, at a modest profit, to his neighbours.

'Lettuces and carrots,' said Mrs Oliver, looking appreciativly at the fine crop of vegetables in her husband's plot. 'Lettuces and carrots. Just right for rabbits. I've always wanted to breed Angoras.'

And before Mr Oliver could say, 'I'm not having any danged rabbits on my property,' his wife had invested some of her life savings in two fine Angoras and a big hutch.

'I'll sell the littl'uns at a handsome profit,' she said, when the doe became pregnant, 'and if I'm lucky, some of them may be good enough to show in competitions and things. I'd rather like to have prize Angoras. Maybe I'll become famous.' And she glowed with pride at the thought.

Sarah awaited the birth with as much excitement as Mrs Oliver and when the kittens arrived she visited them daily, peering through the hole in the top of the hutch and longing for the moment when she could pick up the little creatures and cuddle them.

At one week old the kittens started to grow fur but their eyes were still tightly shut and their tiny ears flattened against their heads.

At the end of the second week, Mrs Oliver allowed Sarah to reach into the nest and take them out one by one. They had grown a coat of soft, white fur and their eyes were wide open, clear and bright.

'They're—oh, they're darling,' Sarah crooned, rubbing them against her cheeks.

'Should fetch a good price too,' added Mrs Oliver, who was of a more practical turn of mind. 'I could get as much as—hello!' She stopped short, looking at one of the kittens in dismay. 'Oh dear,' she said, examining it more closely. 'Oh dear.'

'What's wrong?'

'Its back leg. Look, it's deformed.'

Sarah looked closely. And sure enough the tiny leg was twisted, the foot turned in slightly towards the stomach.

'Poor little thing.' Sarah's heart went out to the crippled kitten.

'Oh, it's no use to us,' said Mrs Oliver in disgust. 'We'll never sell it. Father!' She went to the door of the outhouse and raised her voice. 'Father! Come here a minute, will you, dear?'

Mr Oliver appeared and examined the baby rabbit with a grim expression. 'No hope for it,' he said, looking at the misshapen leg. 'And it's a weakling to boot. Look how much smaller it is than the others. It's the runt of the litter. We'll get no joy of that one.'

'What will you do with it?' said Sarah, a horrible thought beginning to form at the back of her mind.

'Why, get rid of it, of course,' said Mrs Oliver matter-of-factly, confirming the girl's suspicions. 'Father will drown it in the rain barrel.'

'Oh no!' Sarah was aghast. 'Oh, please don't kill it. Let me have it. I'll look after it. I promise.'

'It won't live. It's a waste of time trying to rear it.'

'Let me try—please!'

'And what about your mother? You know she's allergic to animal fur. I don't think she'll be very pleased about a long-haired Angora, will she?' protested Mrs Oliver.

'I'll keep it away from her. I'll—I'll keep it in a hutch in the garden. She need never go near it. Please?' Sarah pleaded.

'Oh, all right.' The old woman put the little kitten into the girl's outstretched hands. 'But you're wasting your time,' she added. 'It's a sickly creature. It won't live. You mark my words.'

Sarah carried it back to her bedroom and, wrapping it gently in blankets, she put it in an old dolls' cradle that she used to play with when she was very small. Mrs Marlowe looked at the rabbit askance but she said nothing. She knew Sarah was still very upset about her father leaving and she hoped that caring for the helpless kitten would alleviate some of her pain.

'I'm going to call you Biminy,' Sarah said to the little thing. 'And you're going to live. Do you hear me, Biminy? You're going to live.'

Biminy heard—but the struggle to survive was sometimes too much for his frail body. Sarah fed him all the warm milk he could take from a stopper and the rest of the time she sat by his box, day and night, rocking him and stroking his head, willing him to live with every ounce of strength she possessed.

The kitten waxed and waned. Sometimes he lay, hardly breathing, and Sarah prayed for his life, making all manner of rash promises to God if he would only spare him. It mattered to her intensely, more than anything else in the world, that Biminy should live. He was her rabbit, her pet, her baby. After a while the little creature began to respond to her loving care.

'He's putting on weight,' said Mrs Marlowe encouragingly. 'You should start feeding him solids.'

Biminy's diet was gradually switched from warm milk to tender young lettuce leaves, clover, peas and minced carrots. He grew stronger and bigger. His little cradle cramped his expanding body and inquisitive spirit, so Sarah made him a new home in a much larger box, with a piece cut out of the side as a door, which she kept by her bed all the time. It comforted her, when she woke in the cold, dark hours of the night, to reach out and feel the warm little body, and sometimes, when she had had a particularly nasty nightmare, she took the rabbit into her bed and held him tightly.

'When he gets really big,' her mother warned, 'he'll have to go out in the garden. We'll ask Mr Oliver to make a hutch for him. You can't have a rabbit in your bedroom for ever, you know. It isn't healthy.'

Sarah didn't really care whether it was healthy or not. She loved animals and her idea of happiness was to be near them. When she grew up, she wanted to be a vet. She would live in The Grange and keep all kinds of animals in the grounds—some of them wild ones. She might even make it into a nature reserve, she decided, delighted at the prospect.

Nicholas viewed the baby rabbit with a certain disdain at the beginning and, as Sarah's love for it grew, the boy became strangely resentful.

'What's the matter with Nick these days?' Sarah asked her mother after a particularly vicious quarrel with her brother. 'He's changed.'

Mrs Marlowe nodded sadly. 'I'm afraid he's very bitter about Daddy leaving, darling. He feels angry and frustrated and sad—and he doesn't know how to express it all. Let him work it through. Be patient,' she said, squeezing Sarah's hand.

'But why doesn't he like my rabbit?' persisted Sarah, who was upset and confused by her brother's strange behaviour. 'Biminy hasn't done anything to hurt him. He said the other day, "We ought to kill that coney and have it for Sunday dinner" and Mummy,' Sarah added anxiously, 'I think he meant it. He looked so hateful.'

'He doesn't really,' said Mrs Marlowe, putting her arm around her. 'I think he feels—well, he feels jealous because you have Biminy to love.'

'But he could have a rabbit, Mummy. Mrs Oliver would sell him one. She might even give him one,' said Sarah enthusiastically. 'She really likes Nick, you know. He's always been her favourite.'

But her mother shook her head. 'Rabbits aren't the solution to Nick's problems,' she said quietly. 'It isn't as simple as that.'

'But why?'

'Oh Sarah,' her mother sighed. 'Human beings are complicated.' She looked into the girl's intense face. 'And it's so difficult for little girls to understand, isn't it?' she said, hugging her daughter tightly.

'Will Daddy ever come back to us?' said Sarah in a very small voice.

'No, darling.' Her mother's voice sounded very final. 'He'll never come back to live with us in this house. My marriage to Daddy is finished. We've agreed to go our separate ways.'

Sarah gulped but said nothing.

'Do you find it too terrible to bear?' said her mother after a while.

Sarah shook her head. 'Not as long as I've got you, Mummy,' she said, hugging her tighter.

But her eyes filled with tears.

41

On Saturday morning the sky was as blue as a cornflour and the sun shone warmly on the village of Croxley.

'Oh good,' thought Sarah, leaping out of bed. 'It will be fine for Amanda's birthday party.'

After breakfast she asked her mother if she could go up to The Grange for a while but Mrs Marlowe had other plans for her.

'I want to go into Evesham,' she said. 'I've a lot of shopping to do and somebody has to help me with it.'

'But what about Ni...?' Sarah began, and then changed her mind. It was hopeless asking her brother to do anything these days.

It was a difficult morning. Sarah was so excited about the party she found it hard to concentrate on mundane things like groceries and vegetables, and Mrs Marlowe snapped at her irritably. 'I seem to be repeating everything twice, Sarah,' she fumed. 'I asked you to get a pound of butter and some Cheddar cheese and what do you bring me back? Half a pound of margarine and horrible, smelly Gorgonzola! I mean, really!'

Sarah looked up at her mother, her face a picture of consternation. Mrs Marlowe glared back—and they both burst out laughing.'

'What am I going to do with you, you pickle?' Mrs Marlowe shook her head in mock despair. 'Come on, let's go to The Pantry and have a milk shake. We could both do with a breather.'

But after lunch, a more serious storm started to brew. Nicholas appeared in the living room in dirty jeans and his old leather jacket.

'And where are you off to?' said his mother, lowering her newspaper to stare icily at him.

'I'm going for a bike ride,' said the boy with studied casualness.

'You're not going for a bike ride, Nicholas,' said his mother, her voice ominously controlled. 'Amanda's party starts at three o'clock. It is now two fifteen. You should be upstairs at this very moment showering and getting into some decent clothes.'

Nicholas folded his arms and stood four square in front of his mother, prepared to battle to the death. 'I told you,' he said. 'I'm not going to Amanda's party. She's just a silly little kid. I don't want to go, and you can't make me.'

'Nicholas!' Mrs Marlowe slammed the newspaper down and rose to her feet. Sarah, who had been sitting on the chesterfield, reading, hastily put her book to one side and ran out of the room.

The invitation from The Grange had caused a great deal of misery for the Marlowes, Nicholas protesting that he would not go, and his mother equally determined that he would. The battle raged, on and off, for days.

Sarah ran into the bathroom and closed the door firmly behind her. As quickly as she could, she pulled off her jeans and shirt and stepped into the shower, turning on the water full blast to block out the angry voices raging downstairs. She soaped herself twice, to make her skin as clean and clear as possible. But no matter how hard she scrubbed, she knew she would never have the delicate complexion of her cousin. Amanda was a peaches and cream girl and her long, pale gold hair made her look like a princess out of *Grimm's Fairy*

43

Tales. Sarah longed to be a blond. Her own dark, curly hair and ruddy complexion infuriated her.

'When I grow up,' she would tell her father, 'I'm going to dye my hair blond and wear a lot of make up so that I look very pale and delicate.'

'You're not going to do anything of the sort,' her father would reply indignantly. 'What! Cover up those beautiful apple cheeks!'

As Sarah dried herself she sang at the top of her voice to drown the quarrelling voices. But still they came through.

'I hate them!' Nicholas yelled. 'I hate all of them! They make me absolutely sick! I hate you too! I....'

Sarah turned on the hair dryer and brushed her hair, willing it to lie flat and sleek like Amanda's but it bounced back defiantly.

'You wouldn't push me around if Daddy were still here!'

Sarah's heart missed a beat. It was the first time she had heard Nicholas mention his father. Tiptoeing back to her room, she dressed quickly, stopping only to survey her image in the wardrobe mirror.

'Just let me alone!' Nicholas screamed. 'Get off my back!'

Sarah scooted down the stairs, yelled 'Goodbye!' to her mother and, without waiting for an answer, shot out into the back garden. Biminy was dozing in his hutch but he stirred when he saw Sarah and pricked up his ears hopefully. 'Come on, sweetheart,' she whispered to him, taking him out of the hutch and giving him a little hug. 'We're off to a party.' And she put him in her basket and carried him off to The Grange.

Of course everybody would ask why she had brought her rabbit to the party. She knew that people in the village raised their eyebrows when she walked by with Biminy in a basket on her arm and some of them had spoken to her mother about it, in a wondering kind of way.

'She takes it everywhere with her,' her mother laughingly replied. 'She'd take it into her bed too—if I let her.'

'He's a cripple, you see,' Sarah would explain, showing them Biminy's twisted hind leg. 'So I think he needs special care and attention.'

It had become her stock answer. But she never told anyone the real reason why she carried the big white rabbit wherever she went. It seemed too incredible—too horrible. But the baleful look in her brother's eyes convinced her she was right.

Most of the guests had arrived by the time Sarah got to The Grange. A line of expensive cars were parked in front of the house and there were excited shouts and laughter from inside.

'Sarah, darling, what a pretty dress!' said Aunt Angela, opening the door to her. 'You look absolutely lovely.'

'Do you l-l-like it?' said Sarah, looking down at the long red and white gingham her mother had made for her. They had spent so much time together choosing the right pattern, the prettiest material, the ribbons to go round the sleeves and neck, and Sarah was delighted

45

with her reflection in the long mirror when the dress was finished.

'You'll be the Belle of the Ball,' laughed her uncle, coming to greet her. 'Amanda!' he called. 'Come here a minute, please. You have another guest. Amanda!'

As soon as Sarah saw her cousin, her heart sank.

'Oh,' she said, gaping at the girl. 'Oh, you look so....'

But no words seemed enough to describe Amanda's fragile beauty. She floated towards Sarah in a long, white dress that swirled around her like a cloud. A pale pink sash circled her waist and matching rosebuds adorned her hair, which fell down her back in a shining, golden cascade. Amanda's skin glowed whiter than snow and her eyes, wide with happiness and excitement, were as blue and round as a doll's. A Dresden doll, thought Sarah enviously. And suddenly her own dress didn't seem so pretty any more.

'Happy birthday,' she said, handing her cousin a big box tied with a silver ribbon. 'It isn't...' she began, but checked herself quickly. She had been about to say, 'It isn't as nice as the dolls' house, of course,' but realized just in time that she was not supposed to know about it.

'Oh, thank you.' Amanda ripped open the box and pulled out a brightly coloured patchwork quilt. 'It's lovely. It's just what I've...'

'...always wanted,' laughed her father, cuffing her cheek. 'Don't be so corny, love.'

Sometimes he seemed a little exasperated at his daughter's rather genteel ways.

'But it is nice,' said Aunt Angela, admiring the quilt. 'Did your mother make it, Sarah? What a clever woman she is. I should take lessons from her.'

'Come on,' Amanda said, pulling at her cousin impatiently. 'All my friends are here.'

46

'Let me take Biminy from you.' Uncle Ted reached out for the basket but Sarah drew back. 'You don't want to carry him everywhere, sweetheart,' said the man, coaxing the basket from her. 'I'll put him somewhere safe. Promise.'

'Where?'

'In the conservatory. He'll be quite all right in there. Nobody will go near him.'

Sarah gave in reluctantly. Protecting the rabbit had become second nature to her now, even when Nicholas wasn't around.

She followed Amanda into the long, oak-panelled lounge which seemed to be full of people, mainly children, rushing around, for the most part, screaming their heads off. Amanda was immediately whisked away by a group of girls who clustered round her whispering and giggling.

Sarah stepped back shyly, feeling awkward and out of place, and trod heavily on someone's foot. 'Oh s-s-sorry,' she stammered, spinning round.

'Don't mention it,' said her cousin William, who was leaning against the wall, a look of great boredom on his face.

'They're playing silly games,' he said, drawing Sarah to one side. 'They're such babies,' he added with the lofty contempt of a twelve-year-old for his younger sister and her friends.

'Shall we go and play chess?' he suggested, his face brightening at the thought. 'Nobody will notice if we just disappear. And we can come back at tea time.'

'Certainly not.' Sarah laughed, appalled at the idea. 'It would be terribly rude.'

Her cousin shrugged. 'Well, I'm going anyway. I've had enough of this.'

Sarah followed him into the hall and peeked round the door of the study, where most of the grown-ups seemed to have gathered.

'Hello, Sarah. How are you, darling?' said a large, red-faced man, stooping to kiss her.

'Oh, hello, Uncle Frank. I'm fine.'

There were lots of Sarah's aunts and uncles in the study and some distant relatives she only seemed to see at Christmas and birthday parties. All had to be greeted and kissed and for the next hour the girl was absorbed in conversations which invariably began with, 'My, how you've grown!' and 'How much taller are you going to get?' This was usually followed by, 'And where is Nicholas? Isn't he coming?'

The first question was easy to answer. It was silly, anyway, but adults seemed fascinated by the speed with which children grew, as if it were some miracle. The second question was trickier. Where *was* Nicholas, Sarah wondered? Still at home, quarrelling with his mother? Sulking in his room? Riding furiously round the countryside on his bike? Of one thing she was sure—he would never come to The Grange.

After a while, when the noise of the party had reached a crescendo, Mr Allen went into the hall and, picking up a beater, he struck a huge brass gong which stood in one corner. Its sonorous echo reverberated through the house. Everybody stopped what they were doing or saying and turned, open-mouthed, towards their host.

'Ladies and gentlemen,' he shouted. 'Tea is now being served in the marquee. Will you please...?' But the rest of the sentence was drowned in the hubbub as the guests all headed for the garden, the children galloping ahead, squealing with joy.

It was a red and white marquee with red flags and

49

streamers fluttering from both ends and across the entrance a big banner which said, 'Happy Birthday Amanda.' Inside there were long tresselled tables covered with white damask cloths and heaped with all kinds of delicious things to eat. Banks of pink and white carnations filled the air with their heavy perfume and soft music wafted from speakers set high in the roof. Waitresses with frilly aprons and starched white caps moved among the guests offering wine, for the adults, and fresh orange juice and lemonade for the children.

On the centre table stood Amanda's birthday cake, a magnificent three-tiered confection on a silver stand.

'What do you think of that, then?' said Uncle Frank, standing back to admire it. 'Big enough to feed the whole of the Russian army, I'd say. I hope it's a fruit cake. Is it?' he asked one of the waitresses. But she shook her head.

'I think it's sponge, sir, with a lemon cream filling.'

'Oh well,' Uncle Frank shrugged. 'It looks good, anyway.'

'It's just beautiful,' breathed Sarah. 'Look at the icing,' she said, pointing to the intricate scrolls and petals covering the cake. 'And the rosebuds—aren't they pretty?'

'Mmm,' agreed her uncle. 'They match the flowers in Amanda's hair.'

'So they do!' Sarah was enchanted. 'What a lovely idea.'

She looked around her, at the warm sunlight pouring through the door of the marquee, the bright green grass beneath her feet, the flowers, the silver and crystal glittering on the tables, the pink and white perfection of the cake, the pretty clothes on the young girls, the happy faces of the guests. 'This place is like fairyland,'

50

she said. And then, out of the corner of her eye, she suddenly saw Nicholas.

And the spell was broken.

He was standing by his mother just inside the door of the marquee and the scowl on his face was enough to freeze a flame.

Sarah turned away quickly. She wasn't going to let her brother spoil the lovely day.

'But it must be awfully inconvenient for you, living so far from Birmingham,' one of her relatives was saying to Uncle Ted.

'Not at all, it's only an hour's drive. I'm in the office by eight thirty every morning.'

'But don't you feel terribly cut off here?' the woman persisted. 'I mean, village life can be so deadly dull when you're used to city living.'

'Village life is marvellous, believe me. There's plenty to do around here.' Mr Allen was determinedly enthusiastic.

'And what about the children's schooling?'

'They'll go to the same schools. Fortunately they take boarders.'

'But don't you...?'

Sarah frowned and moved away. Silly woman, she thought, taking a couple of chocolate éclairs and retiring to a quiet corner of the marquee.

'Hello, darling.' It was her mother. 'Enjoying yourself?' Sarah nodded enthusiastically.

'But why are you all alone? Where's...?' Her mother looked around the marquee. 'Where's Amanda?'

'Oh, she's off somewhere with her school friends.' Sarah dismissed it casually. 'She's all excited about seeing them again. Everybody likes my dress,' she said, to take her mother's mind off the subject.

51

'I should think so too,' said Mrs Marlowe. 'You look really pretty.'

Sarah looked at her mother. 'So do you,' she said.

Sarah had never really noticed her mother before her father left. Mrs Marlowe was just, well, there—keeping the house clean, cooking, comforting her children when they hurt themselves, but not really a person, Sarah thought, not like old Mr Haines—a real character—or her father. Oh, of course she knew her mother was a pretty woman, very pretty when she was happy and smiling, but she had always been rather dull, wearing clothes that seemed to fade her into the background— colourless sweaters, nondescript skirts and sensible walking shoes. Since the breakup of her marriage and her return to work, however, Mrs Marlowe had changed abruptly. She had her reddish brown hair cut short and permed. She started to wear make up—even Nicholas noticed the difference—and the sweaters and sensible shoes were exchanged for brightly coloured dresses and high-heeled shoes.

'That's a new dress, isn't it?' said Sarah, looking at her mother with pride. 'It's lovely.'

'Thank you, darling.' Mrs Marlowe leaned forward and kissed her. She smelt delicious too, Sarah thought, the way Mrs Hamilton de Vere used to when she rode off in her Daimler. 'You're sweet,' she added, giving her daughter a hug.

'I see Nick came,' Sarah said.

Immediately her mother's face set in a stern expression. 'I only hope he'll behave himself,' she muttered through clenched teeth. 'He's in a very silly, rebellious mood.'

Sarah could see her brother at the other side of the marquee. He was surrounded by a group of doting aunts, all of whom were asking the same, inevitable questions. From the look on his face, Sarah thought, Nicholas was obviously tolerating their prattle quite well, though his answers appeared to be very brief.

'Stella.' Uncle Frank advanced on Mrs Marlowe with a purposeful look. 'I was really sorry to hear about Robert leaving you, my dear. I suppose you'll divor....' He paused and looked doubtfully at Sarah. Then, taking her mother by the elbow, he led her discreetly away, talking earnestly all the while.

Sarah sighed and stared at her empty plate. Nobody had spoken to her about her father but they had all asked questions with their eyes. They looked at her as if they were searching for scars or some outward sign of inward distress.

'How's the business then?' boomed a large, jovial man, slapping Mr Allen on the shoulder. Sarah didn't recognize him, but she imagined he was one of Aunt Angela's relatives. 'On to the second million, are we?' he guffawed.

Mr Allen winced and looked round, as if seeking escape.

'Ah, Sarah!' He beckoned her to him. 'Go and find Amanda, will you, love? Tell her it's time to cut the cake. Excuse me a minute, Arthur,' he said to the other man, 'I must just have a word with one of the waitresses about...' and he melted into the crowd.

Sarah put down her plate and walked round the marquee, looking for Amanda. Nicholas made a face at her as she passed and William was standing by himself, looking patently bored. But Amanda was nowhere to be seen. Sarah wandered out into the grounds, calling her cousin loudly.

'I think she's in the house, dear,' said one of her aunts

helpfully. And so she was, showing off the new dolls' house to a group of admiring friends.

'Daddy had it especially made for me by a man in London. You see, he's copied everything exactly, even the....' She paused as Sarah whispered Mr Allen's message in her ear. 'Oh yes, the cake!' she cried, springing to her feet. 'Come on, everybody, I'm going to cut my cake!'

Sarah followed her down the stairs, surrounded by a group of chattering, giggling girls, but on the way back to the marquee she suddenly remembered Biminy.

'Bet Uncle Ted put him on the window ledge in the conservatory,' she thought. And sure enough the rabbit was there, all scrunched up in his basket in a contented kind of way, obviously thinking happy rabbity thoughts.

'I'll bring you a lettuce leaf,' Sarah whispered, tickling him behind the ear. 'Won't be long,' she added, lest the rabbit should pine. 'I'm going to have a piece of Amanda's lovely birthday cake and then I'll come back.'

But as soon as she stepped out of the house, Sarah sensed that something had gone terribly wrong. Bad, sad vibrations emanated from the marquee. People spoke in shocked, hushed voices.

'What's wrong? What's happened?' Sarah cried, pushing her way through the crowd.

Amanda was sobbing in her father's arms. Aunt Angela was standing beside them, murmuring words of comfort, and everybody else was standing around in an embarrassed kind of way.

'What's happened?' Sarah demanded, getting quite angry because nobody would answer her question.

Uncle Ted shook his head and pointed to the table where the magnificent cake stood. But it was magnificent no longer. The top tier and half of the second and third tiers were crushed and battered. The icing was all broken, the creamy sponge oozed through, and the delicate pink rosebuds were scattered all over the tablecloth and floor.

'Oh!' Sarah could scarcely believe her eyes. What had been all pristine beauty a few minutes ago was now an unappetizing mess. 'How did it happen?' she asked in amazement.

'I'm afraid your brother did it,' said Uncle Frank.

Sarah spun round to face him. 'Oh n–n–no!' she protested, in defence of Nicholas.

'Oh yes,' said the man firmly, looking very angry.

Sarah turned to Aunt Angela in bewilderment. Nicholas and her mother were nowhere in sight. 'Apparently he was reaching for a plate or a cup or something,' her aunt explained, 'and lost his balance and fell heavily against the cake. It was an unfortunate accident.'

'A very unfortunate accident,' Uncle Frank repeated. 'That young man should be careful where he falls in the future,' he added grimly, 'or he may end up in serious trouble.'

Sarah never found out what happened between her mother and brother that afternoon but when she got home from the party the atmosphere in the house was icy.

'Mummy, do you really think that Nick...?' began Sarah, but Mrs Marlowe only shook her head and

55

turned away, too distressed to talk about it.

As for Nicholas, he stayed in his room, emerging only for meals, which he ate in sulky silence.

Nothing was said at The Grange either.

'It doesn't matter,' shrugged Amanda.

'Who cares?' said William breezily, feigning indifference.

And life returned to normal, the way it always does, no matter what calamity has happened. Mr Allen went back to work, Sarah went to The Grange to play with Amanda's new dolls' house, and Nicholas tore round the country lanes on his bike pretending he was riding a great Triumph 650 motor bike, his eyes gleaming at the thought.

He had found a new friend too. Sarah, wandering home from The Grange later that week, humming happily to herself, suddenly came face to face with Nicholas and another boy.

'Oh, it's you,' said Nicholas, dismissing her from his presence as if she were an insect.

Sarah prepared to walk by but the strange boy stepped in front of her, blocking her way.

'Who's she then?' he said, looking down at the girl in a contemptuous way.

Sarah cowered away from him. He was big, much bigger than Nicholas, with a surly face covered in angry boils and spots. His black, greasy hair hung to his shoulders and he constantly flicked it away from his face in a gesture that was almost a nervous tic.

'She's my sister,' said Nicholas. 'And that stupid, lop-eared thing in her basket is her pet rabbit.'

Sarah put the basket behind her back.

'Let me see it,' said the boy.

'No.'

''Ere, don't you answer me back.' His voice was menacing. 'When I tell you to do somethin', you do it fast, understand? Now, show me that rabbit.'

Sarah looked desperately at Nicholas but he stood to one side, surveying the scene with amusement. Her heart pounding furiously, she stepped towards the boy and offered up the basket but, just as he reached in, she gave him a swift, hard kick in the shins.

'Ow! Ow!' He let out a roar of pain and grabbed his ankle. 'You little…!'

Sarah dodged past him and ran down the lane as fast as she could.

'Just wait till I get you! I'll—I'll…!'

Feet came pounding after her. 'Leave her alone, Eddie!' Sarah heard her brother shout after the boy. 'Come on, we've got other things to do!'

The footsteps died away and Sarah ran on, too frightened to stop. When she was safely back in her home, she locked and bolted the front door. Then she ran round the house, hysterically closing windows lest Nicholas and the horrible boy should try to get in.

'They won't touch you, Biminy. I won't l-l-let them touch you,' she comforted the startled rabbit. And then, burying her head in his soft fur, she wept. 'If only Mummy were here,' she sobbed, feeling very lonely and afraid. 'If only M-M-Mummy were here.'

But Mrs Marlowe would not be back until the early evening. She had taken a job in Cheltenham after her husband left for the Middle East, a job that took up more and more of her time.

'It isn't that I need the money especially; Daddy sends us enough to live on,' she had explained to a puzzled Sarah and Nicholas, 'but I want to get out of the house, meet people, make new friends.'

Sarah had frowned. 'But you have us....'

'Of course I do, darling'—her mother swept her into her arms and hugged her tightly—'and I love you both very much, you know that. It's just that—oh, how can I explain it—I'm an adult and I miss the company of other adults. I like to talk about things like, well, politics, the kind of things that bore you, anyway. When Daddy was here, it was all right, but....' Her voice petered out.

'But you have Uncle Ted and Aunt Angela,' persisted Sarah. 'That's why they moved down here, didn't they?'

'Yes, they did, darling,' her mother agreed. 'And I really appreciate having them close by. Uncle Ted has been a tower of strength to me and Aunt Angela is the kindest person in the world. But I can't rely on them for companionship all the time, can I? I have my own life to lead, my own friends to make. I have things I want to do by myself....'

'Sounds boring to me,' said Nicholas rather petulantly, referring to his mother's new job. 'Why don't you do something exciting instead of working in a dull old shop?'

'You could be a buyer for a big shop like you used to,' cut in Sarah enthusiastically. 'That would be fun!'

'Indeed it would,' her mother laughed. 'And how do you think I could travel round the country or go abroad for weeks at a time and leave you two alone here?'

'We'd be good,' said Nicholas.

'Good?' his mother echoed incredulously. 'Young man, I'm even afraid to leave you to your own devices for one morning, let alone a whole week. Mischief has become your middle name.'

Nicholas reddened.

'Anyway'—Mrs Marlowe's mind was made up—'being a shop assistant will suit me very well until you're both

58

grown up and off my hands. Then I'll find something more glamorous,' she added, for Nick's benefit. 'If you need me, you can phone me at Bendall's. Here's my number. But it must be something urgent, do you understand? I don't want to be disturbed every half hour with idle chatter.'

The children nodded.

'And don't look so tragic, Sarah. It's only a part-time job. I'll be home by the time you get back from school every day. You won't even know I'm not here.'

And it was true, of course. The three of them left the house at the same time every morning, Nicholas to his school the other side of Cheltenham, Sarah to the local girls' school and Mrs Marlowe to her job at Bendall's. By the time the children returned in the afternoon, their mother was already home, preparing the evening meal.

Everything went smoothly for a while, and then the system began to fall apart. Mrs Marlowe's part-time job became full-time and, with the advent of the long summer holidays, the children were at home all day, alone.

Nicholas with time on his hands and nobody to restrain him became a very unpleasant boy and Sarah avoided him as much as she could, escaping to The Grange to play with Amanda and William or wander round the grounds chatting with the gardeners.

Nicholas was lonely. He had dropped all his old friends and given up his hobbies.

'Don't see that there brother of yours no more,' said Mr Haines to Sarah one day. 'Used ter love beaglin', 'e did. Couldn't get enough of it. All weathers 'e were out—couldn't keep 'im at 'ome. Now,' the old man shrugged in bewilderment, 'now 'e don't want to know me no more. I sees 'im the other mornin'. "'Ere, Nick," I says to 'im, "we're off with the 'ounds termorrow. Are you comin' then?" But 'e looks daggers at me—as if I'd upset 'im or somethin'. So I thinks to meself best leave young Nicholas alone.'

And everybody in the village thought the same.

'I see your brother has taken up with Eddie Lewis,' said Farmer Bancroft, when Sarah went over to ride his ponies. 'If I were you, I'd advise Nicholas to stay away from that young man. He's a nasty character, a real troublemaker.'

'Do you know him then?' said Sarah, who had never seen the boy before.

The farmer nodded. 'He comes from the new estate on the other side of the highway. Moved there from London with his family last year, I believe. I know him— or know of him, anyway—because he used to go to the Rose and Crown with some other louts. They'd all roar up on those damned motor bikes and make thorough nuisances of themselves. But Dick Morris won't let them in any more.'

'Why?'

'They had a fight one night, smashed furniture and glasses, and threatened to harm Dick himself if he interfered. In fact, if I remember rightly, it was Eddie Lewis who tried to push a broken bottle in Dick's face.'

Sarah was horrified.

'Dick called the police, of course,' the farmer went on. 'Terrible scene. Now he's bought a couple of Doberman pinschers as guard dogs. Fierce brutes they are, too. Dick says if those boys ever go near his pub again, he'll set the dogs on them and to hell with the consequences.'

Sarah relayed the story to her mother.

'I know, love.' Mrs Marlowe shook her head in despair. 'I've seen Nick with that awful boy and I made some enquiries about him. He's eighteen years old, apparently. Eighteen! Why would a boy of that age want to hang around with a little kid like Nick?'

'Perhaps it's Nick who wants to hang around with him?' suggested Sarah.

Her mother nodded. 'You're probably right. He seems determined to get into trouble and, from all that I've heard about Eddie Lewis, he's in the right company now. I just don't know what to do about it....' She sat for a long time, gazing into space.

'Perhaps'—Sarah hesitated to make the suggestion but she plunged ahead anyway—'perhaps Daddy could do something. If you wrote to him and told him the way Nick's behaving, he might....' But a loud knock at the front door interrupted her.

'The paper boy, probably,' said Mrs Marlowe, rising wearily from her seat. 'Go and get my purse, darling. It's in my bedroom on the dressing table.'

Sarah ran upstairs while her mother went to open the door.

'Good evening, Mrs Marlowe.'

Sarah recognized the voice instantly. It was the village constable, John Fulton. She ran down the stairs again and stood by her mother.

'Hello, Sarah,' said the policeman, smiling pleasantly. 'How are you?'

'I'm O.K., thanks,' said Sarah, wondering what on earth Constable Fulton wanted with them.

'Is something wrong?' said Mrs Marlowe. 'Don't tell me I've parked my car in the wrong place again?' She laughed nervously.

But the policeman didn't laugh. He shook his head. 'I'm afraid we've had a spot of bother—with that lad of yours.'

61

Sarah had a sickly feeling in her stomach and she put her hand in her mother's.

'Nicholas? What has he done?' Mrs Marlowe went white and squeezed Sarah's hand convulsively.

'It seems he and another boy got into a fight with young Jimmy Spender and broke his guitar. Smashed it, they did, beyond repair.'

'Have you—did you . . . ? Mrs Marlowe couldn't find the words.

'We caught Nicholas,' the policeman nodded, 'but the other boy got away—ran across the fields.'

'I know who it is!' Sarah blurted out.

'So do I,' said Constable Fulton grimly. 'And I suggest you tell Nicholas to stay away from the likes of him. He's a bad lot, that one.'

'What will you do with N–N–N . . . ?' Sarah stammered.

'Nothing this time.' The policeman smiled and put a comforting hand on the girl's head. 'But if he gets into mischief again'—he looked sternly at Mrs Marlowe—'I shan't be so lenient with him.'

Mrs Marlowe made Nicholas pay for Jimmy Spender's guitar. He emptied all the money out of his savings box and went to work for Farmer Bancroft every morning to make up the balance.

'You can pick plums, dig ditches, clean out the pig pens for all I care,' his mother fumed. 'I hope he gives

you hard work, really hard work, Nicholas, so the next time you're tempted to smash somebody's property you'll think twice about it. And another thing,' she raged, 'I don't want that wretched Eddie Lewis in my house ever again, do you understand? If I even see him near my property, I'll call the police and have him arrested for trespassing.'

Nicholas stared at the floor, his expression defiant, but he said nothing.

'I don't understand why you did such a thing,' Mrs Marlowe repeated for the umpteenth time. 'Jimmy Spender used to be such a good friend of yours. And you know how much he loved his guitar—you even played it yourself sometimes.'

She stopped pacing the room and looked at her son intently, as if she were willing the answers out of the mute boy.

'Did he say or do something that offended you? I mean, Nick, for goodness' sake, you don't just break a boy's guitar for fun, do you?' she beseeched him.

Nicholas glared back at her.

'He's a creep!' he muttered.

'A creep!' his mother echoed in disgust. 'Nick, even your language is slipping into the gutter.'

'Used to be such a nice boy, your brother,' Farmer Bancroft said to Sarah the next time she paid him a visit. 'But now....' He shook his head. 'I can't even get a good morning out of him. I'm only letting him work here as a favour to your mother. I wouldn't have such a sullen person around me otherwise.'

'He should go to boarding school,' said Uncle Ted. 'Best thing for him.'

'But it's much too late for this year,' protested Mrs Marlowe. 'School starts in a few weeks. I should have applied months ago. And anyway....' She wrung her hands in an agony of indecision. 'I'm not so sure that's the right thing for Nicholas. He's terribly troubled. He needs....'

'He needs a good thrashing, that's what he needs,' stormed Farmer Bancroft later that evening. 'He let the bull out of its pen and it went on a fine old rampage all over the farmyard and out into the fields. Took us hours to catch it. Here!' He slammed twenty pounds on the table and walked towards the door. 'There's the money for two weeks' work. Tell him I don't ever want to see him on my farm again. In fact, I'd pay him to stay away!'

Sarah wrote to her father that night, a long letter telling him all about Nicholas and the trouble he was constantly getting into. She had never spoken to anyone about her brother before, and certainly never to her father. Her letters to Mr Marlowe had always been bright and cheerful. She wrote often, filling the pages with newsy details of village life and school. Her mother's letters were brief and factual, she suspected. And as for Nicholas, he never wrote at all.

She posted the letter the following morning, saying a little prayer under her breath as she put it in the box by the village store.

'Uncle Ted phoned,' said her mother when she got home. 'He has a surprise for you. You're to go up to The Grange after lunch.'

'What is it? What is it?' cried Sarah excitedly.

But her mother only laughed. 'If I told you, it wouldn't be a surprise, would it?'

'May I go now?'

'No, you'll just have to contain your curiosity for a few hours.'

'Is it—is it something really nice, Mummy?'

65

Mrs Marlowe nodded. 'It certainly is.'

'Is it just for me?'

'No, it's for all of you.'

'What do you mean—all?' Sarah frowned.

'It's for you and Nicholas and your cousins too. A kind of group present.'

'Is it a ...?'

'No more questions,' said Mrs Marlowe firmly. 'Wait until after lunch and you'll find out for yourself.'

Sarah's eyes shone. 'May we have lunch now?'

'Sarah! It's only ten o'clock. Now go and play with your rabbit or something.'

Sarah wandered out into the garden. To her surprise, Nicholas was leaning nonchalantly against the fence, chewing a blade of grass.

'What are you doing here?' she said, frowning.

'What d'you mean "What am I doing here"? I just happen to live here, in case you've forgotten.'

'I had,' Sarah retorted. 'You're never around.'

'Not like little Miss Goody Two Shoes,' he mimicked his sister's light voice, 'always helping Mummy around the house, doing what she's told, running little errands to uncle and aunty at The Grange. And what are you doing here, anyway?' His voice changed to a growl. 'Oh, of course,' he scoffed, as his sister opened the rabbit hutch and lifted Biminy out, 'we've come to play with our bunny wunny, haven't we?'

Sarah stroked the rabbit, running her fingers through his fur, then she put him on the grass and let him run free.

'You forgot to kiss him,' Nicholas jeered. But the girl busied herself with cleaning the hutch and ignored her brother.

'You should be very careful with that rabbit,' he

cautioned, determined to upset her. 'There's still a lot of myxomatosis about, you know,' he said, moving closer to her so that she could hear him better. 'Have you ever seen a myxie rabbit, Sarah?' he enquired innocently.

Sarah cleaned the inside of the hutch while Biminy lolloped around the garden like a three-legged stool, delighted with his temporary freedom. Usually she swabbed the hutch with disinfectant and scrubbed it, but, since she was anxious to get away from her tormenting brother, she simply brushed it vigorously, working as quickly as she could.

'It's a horrible sight,' Nicholas continued, still on the subject of myxomatosis. 'Apparently their heads swell up like balloons and they go blind and deaf. Oh, and their bottoms swell too. Must be terribly painful, mustn't it? Eddie says he's seen rabbits with myxie....'

Sarah put clean straw in Biminy's cage and a handful of white clover, his favourite food.

'They wander round the countryside.' Nicholas was enjoying himself. 'Can't see their way back to their burrows, apparently, so they die on the road, all alone. Sad, isn't it?'

Sarah picked up Biminy and hugged him tightly.

'I hope he doesn't get it,' Nicholas said. 'We'd have to kill him to put him out of his misery, wouldn't we?'

Sarah put the rabbit back in its hutch, closed the door and went back into the house, ignoring Nicholas completely.

'Mummy,' she said, 'do you think I could keep Biminy in my room—now that the winter's coming?'

'Certainly not. That rabbit's got a perfectly good fur coat on him. He'll withstand the cold better than you will.'

'But....'

'No "buts" Sarah,' Mrs Marlowe said firmly. 'It's unhygienic—and, in any case, I don't want rabbit fur all over the place. You know I'm allergic to it.'

'But Mummy....'

'Sarah!'

'Oh, all right.' The girl stomped up to her room, defeated. Damn her mother's allergy, she thought angrily. It had stopped her from having all kinds of pets. She could have had one of Mrs Hazeldeane's ginger cats and Mr Haines had even offered her one of his beagle pups. And oh, how she longed for a pony of her own. But it was always her mother who said no, no, no. She was allergic to them and, anyway, they were very expensive to keep.

'Excuses, excuses,' grumbled Sarah, wandering over to the window aimlessly. 'She doesn't like animals at all. That's the real reason she won't let me have them. She's a—oh no!' She let out a gasp of horror.

Nicholas was crouched down in front of Biminy's cage, his face against the wire netting.

Sarah pushed open her window and leaned out.

'Nick, leave him alone!' she cried frantically. 'Don't touch him. D–d–don't...!'

The boy rose slowly to his feet and leered up at his sister, feet spread apart, hands on hips in a defiant gesture.

'Keep your hair on, G–G–Goody Two Shoes,' he mocked. 'I was just looking at the stupid animal, that's all. There's no law against it, is there?'

After lunch Sarah went up to The Grange. And, to her amazement, Nicholas went as well.

'So what?' he muttered, stalking along beside her, hands thrust deeply in pockets. 'I might as well see what silly gimmick Uncle Ted has thought up this time.'

But Sarah smiled to herself. Nicholas, despite his outward display of indifference, was intrigued. He wanted to know what the surprise was just as much as his sister, but it had become almost a code of honour with him not to show any enthusiasm about anything.

The labradors came bounding to meet them as usual and Nick bent down to pet and play with them. Sarah stood to one side, holding Biminy behind her back. They were lovely dogs, good-natured and friendly, but she didn't trust them where rabbits were concerned. And Biminy obviously didn't trust them either. He twitched and jumped nervously as soon as he caught wind of them.

'Good boy, Kaly, good boy!' Nicholas scuffled with the dogs, which bounded and leaped around him. 'Do you want something to eat? Dinner? Dinner?'

They barked furiously at the magic word.

'Go on Kaly! Go on, Trot! There's something tasty in Sarah's basket. Dinner, Kaly, dinner!' He provoked the confused animals, pointing to the basket behind Sarah's back.

The girl took a step away, her face contorted with rage. 'Nicholas, you're s–s–sick!' she spat out in disgust.

'Go on, Trot! Dinner! Dinner!' yelled her brother,

69

enjoying her discomfort. 'Go get it! Go get it!' he urged them.

The dogs barked, Nicholas roared with laughter and Sarah shouted, 'Stop it! Nick, stop it!' at the top of her voice.

'Good grief!' Mr Allen suddenly appeared round the side of the house, with his hands over his ears. 'What on earth's going on?'

'It's N–N–Nicholas,' Sarah cried, running to him. 'He's trying to s–set the dogs on B–B–Biminy.'

'Oh, of course he's not, Sarah,' said her uncle reassuringly, calming the dogs with a word. 'He's only teasing you. Why do you let him get at you all the time?'

'He never stops!' Sarah protested. 'He's just r–r–rotten to me.'

'R–r–rotten?' echoed Nicholas, doubling up with laughter again.

'Nick, that's enough!' Mr Allen rounded on him sharply and the boy flinched with surprise. 'Your sister's very upset. Surely you can see that? And it isn't anything to laugh at!' he shouted as Nicholas started to giggle again in an embarrassed kind of way. 'People don't stammer because they're happy and confident, you know. Stammering is a sign of nerves—just like your stupid behaviour these days. If you had any sense at all, you'd know that Sarah is just as unhappy as you— but she doesn't go around behaving like a fool all the time.'

The boy flushed and hung his head.

'Well, come on then.' Mr Allen seemed agitated, as if he regretted what he had said. 'Let's go round the back. The kids are waiting for us.' Sarah took his hand and walked beside him but her brother dragged along behind, kicking the gravel with the toe of his shoe. His face was still red and his mouth set in an angry, sulky line.

Sarah felt close to tears but she held them back. She had never seen her uncle angry before, but what he had said was true—both she and her brother were very unhappy people. She would have liked to talk to Nicholas about it, to discuss it, the way they used to talk about things in the old days. She had tried so often but now he rejected her. He seemed to prefer his own little world of loneliness and misery and every time she mentioned their father he growled at her angrily or, worse, turned away as if he hadn't heard.

William and Amanda were waiting for them by the kitchen garden. The moment she set eyes on her, Sarah knew Amanda was bubbling over with excitement. She could hardly keep still and as soon as she saw her father she blurted out anxiously, 'Have you told them what it is? Have you told them?'

'Of course I have,' her father teased her. 'They know all about it.'

'Oh Daddy, you didn't, did you? Oh that was mean— why did you tell them and not us? Oh did he, Sarah?'

Mr Allen winked at Sarah to keep quiet, but she couldn't help giggling.

'It's all right, Amanda. He hasn't told us a thing,' she comforted her cousin.

'Give us a clue, please,' persisted Amanda, who was beside herself with curiosity. 'Is it big or small? What colour is it? What letter does it begin with?'

'Wait and see,' said Mr Allen.

'Is it a tree house, Daddy? Oh, I'd love a tree house. Or new bikes or...?' Amanda chattered on.

William fell in beside Nicholas.

'Girls are so crazy,' he laughed. 'She's been raving

like this ever since she got out of bed this morning. Lord knows why—but you only have to mention a surprise or a secret to Amanda and she goes right round the bend.'

Nicholas grunted something inaudible in reply.

'Are you going to the cricket match on Saturday, Nick? Croxley is playing Verton in the Village League.' William wasn't really interested in cricket; in fact, he didn't much care for any sport, but he knew Nicholas liked the game and was very good at it.

'No.' The answer was curt.

'I hear the Verton team are pretty sharp this year. Do you think they'll beat us?'

'Don't know.'

'Have you played any cricket lately, Nick?'

'No.'

William sighed and moved away. Without being told, he knew his father wanted him to make a special effort to be friends with Nicholas but it was an uphill task and one that William's heart wasn't really in. He had plenty of good friends at school and he was beginning to make friends with some of the children in the village, so he had no need of his sullen, unsociable cousin.

'This way,' said Mr Allen, leading them all in the direction of the stables. Amanda and Sarah exchanged glances. As they drew near, Sarah picked up the delicious smell of hay and leather and tack that still hung around from the days when the Hamilton de Veres had stabled their piebald ponies there.

'Jim!' Mr Allen paused outside the stable, bringing them all to a halt with his raised hand. 'Jim!' he called again. 'Is it all ready?'

'Oi,' a country voice answered. 'All ready, sir. Shall I bring um out now?'

'Yes please.'

Sarah heard the ring of horses' hooves on the stable floor and her heart turned over. The next moment a beautiful chestnut pony appeared pulling a black, shiny trap.

'Oh!' Sarah was speechless.

'Daddy, it's beautiful.' Amanda's eyes sparkled. 'Where did you get it?'

'I had it made by a company in Winchcombe. They've been making carriages for centuries, apparently. And a lovely job they've done, I must admit.'

The children gathered round to pat the pony and admire the handsome trap harnessed to it.

'Incidentally,' Mr Allen pointed to the boy who stood rather shyly at the pony's head. 'This is Jim Neeld. He's our new stable boy.'

'He is not!' Amanda corrected her father vigorously. 'He's one of the gardeners—he helps Tom with the vegetables and things.'

The boy giggled and hung his head.

'All right, all right,' Mr Allen laughed. 'As from today, Jim is our stable boy-cum-assistant gardener. Does that suit you, madam?' he enquired of his precise daughter.

'What's the horse's name, Uncle Ted?' said Sarah, who was far more interested in the pony than the stable boy.

'He doesn't have one yet. He's waiting for someone to christen him.'

'He must have come with a name, Daddy,' Amanda corrected him again. 'He can't just have been an "it".'

'No, I'm sure he wasn't. But I think we should rechristen him. After all, he's going to be our pony from now on.'

The children looked at each other.

'Dobbin,' said Amanda without a moment's thought.

But the others groaned.

'Can't you do better than that?' chided her brother.

'Well, clever dick, you think of something then.'

'Brandy,' he said.

'Brandy!' scoffed Amanda. 'Gosh, it must have really strained you to think that one up. How unusual!'

'Now come on, you two. Let's not get into a fight about it,' chided their father. 'Sarah...?'

Sarah shook her head and looked at Nicholas. He was feigning indifference but his eyes were taking in all the details of the trap and she knew he was longing to get in it.

'Nick,' she said, 'can you think of a name?'

'Bucephalus,' he said, without hesitation.

'Bu...what?' Amanda frowned.

'Bucephalus,' Nicholas repeated, with a touch of disdain in his voice. 'Alexander the Great's horse.'

'Ah, now there's a proud name for him,' said Mr Allen.

'I think it's a mouthful,' protested Amanda. 'I think we should call him Alexander the Great...Alex for short.'

They all looked at Nicholas, who shrugged.

'I don't care,' he said. 'Call it what you like.'

'Well, get into the trap, all of you,' said Mr Allen briskly. 'Go on, it's big enough for four if you squeeze up,' he said, urging them in.

'Uhm, begging yer pardon, sir, but thur won't be no room fer me,' said Jim Neeld shyly. And he laughed. 'Who's going t'drive if I can't get in?'

'You could sit on Amanda's lap,' suggested Mr Allen, tongue in cheek.

'Daddy!' the girl protested, colouring slightly. Amanda had a very strict code of etiquette, strict to the point of primness, and her father's teasing often offended her.

'Nick,' said Mr Allen, 'you could handle it, couldn't you? He's a very fine horseman, you know,' he added to the stable boy, who looked doubtful. 'Give him the whip, Jim. There you are, Nicholas. Let's see you put Alexander through his paces.'

Nicholas took the whip and held it in his left hand, then, gathering up the reins, he urged the pony forward with a click of his tongue. The chestnut flattened its ears and set off at a trot. The trap lurched, swaying lightly back and forth like a cork on water, and Amanda let out a little shriek.

But Sarah wasn't afraid. 'Isn't it beautiful?' she said, touching the quilted red leather that lined the seats. 'I feel like the Queen riding out of Buckingham Palace in a ... what do you call those carriages, the open ones that look like a baby's pram?'

'Landaus,' said William.

'Yes, that's right.' Sarah raised her right hand and waved regally to the imaginary crowds lining the route. Amanda followed suit, but she kept one hand firmly on the side of the trap and her smile wasn't as relaxed as Sarah's.

'Stay in the grounds, Nick,' shouted his uncle. 'Don't go outside.'

The boy raised his whip to acknowledge the command and brought it down crack, neatly flicking the pony's flanks. Immediately it lunged into a gallop.

'Oh Nick, no!' cried Amanda, holding on to the sides of the trap till her knuckles turned white. 'Slow down!'

'Er ... I think we're a bit out of control,' said William, his face turning ashen as trees and bushes flashed by on either side.

'Course we're not,' scowled Nicholas. 'Look!' And he immediately pulled the pony back to a trot and then to a

75

complete halt.

William looked abashed and Amanda let go of the sides and folded her hands in her lap so that nobody would see them shaking.

'Do you want me to drive or not?' said Nicholas haughtily.

'There's no need to be so smart about it!'

'Oh go on, Nick, stop playing the fool!'

Nicholas set the pony off again at a quiet trot.

'Enjoying it?' cried Mr Allen as they swept by him.

'Great!' they chorused, waving back.

'Daddy,' Amanda called. 'Whose pony and trap is it?'

William made a face. His sister was a very matter-of-fact girl; she liked to know exactly what belonged to her and what didn't.

'It's owned by a consortium,' answered her father.

'A what?'

'A consortium,' he yelled again, cupping his hands around his mouth as the trap sped away down the drive. 'The Marlowes and the Allens equally.'

'What is he talking about?' Amanda turned to her brother.

'He means it belongs to all of us, equal shares,' William explained.

'Oh.' Amanda didn't look very pleased about that.

'Do you think you'll fall apart if I gallop again?' Nicholas said.

The little girl sat up stiffly, her pride hurt. 'Go as fast as you like,' she snapped. 'I don't care.'

Nicholas flicked the whip and away they went. 'Come on, Alexander,' he cried. 'Move!'

'It's like riding on a great wave!' said William, as the highly sprung trap sped along on its two great wheels.

'It's like riding on a cloud!' exclaimed Amanda, who

would really have preferred to be safely on the ground if the truth be told.

'It's—it's like heaven!' Sarah was exhilarated.

Nicholas flicked the whip again.

'Wheeeeeeeee!' cried William. 'Fasten your seat belts, please. We're about to take off.'

Sarah's face glowed with pleasure. 'Isn't this fun, Nick?' she bubbled to her brother, who was concentrating on the narrow path ahead. 'Isn't it marvellous?'

But Nicholas only shrugged. 'Kids' stuff,' he muttered. 'I'd rather have a motor bike any day.'

With the arrival of the pony and trap, Sarah began to spend even more time at The Grange. Jim Neeld taught her to drive and she learned quickly. But her cousins hung back, reluctant to take the reins. They were a little afraid of the pony, though they would never have admitted it, and any speed above a walk set Amanda trembling.

But Sarah was fearless. She adored horses and when she wasn't taking her cousins for a drive in the handsome trap, she saddled Alexander and rode him round the grounds, cantering and galloping to her heart's content. Afterwards she helped Jim Neeld in the stable, feeding hay and oats to Alexander or brushing his thick red coat till it shone.

'Why doesn't Nicholas come?' said Amanda one day, watching Sarah at work. 'He's not had a ride since that very first day. Daddy bought the pony for him as well, you know. We all own Alexander equally,' she added in an accusing tone.

Sarah blushed and, ducking under the pony, she started to brush his belly vigorously, pretending not to have heard her cousin.

'Sarah, I said why doesn't...?' Amanda began again but stopped abruptly at a sharp dig in the ribs from her more astute brother.

Sarah was embarrassed. Nicholas had not been near the stable, had not even mentioned the pony and trap. 'I'm not interested in the silly thing,' he growled when his mother questioned him angrily, accusing him of ingratitude. 'I want a motor bike.'

'Don't be stupid, Nick!' she snapped. 'You're much too young for one of those wretched machines.'

'I can have one when I'm eighteen.'

'Over my dead body!'

'Well, I will, anyway,' said Nicholas insolently. 'Try and stop me!' And he stomped out of the house, slamming the front door after him.

Mrs Marlowe looked at Sarah and raised her hands in a gesture of utter helplessness. 'Well, that idea of Uncle Ted's didn't get us very far, did it?' she said. 'The only person who really enjoys the pony is you and you're no problem to me anyway, are you, darling?' She cupped her hand under Sarah's chin and kissed the girl tenderly.

Sarah did enjoy the pony, but she was beginning to enjoy Jim Neeld's company too. The stable boy was a cheerful companion, full of hilarious stories about the small home where he lived with his parents and six brothers and sisters. Sarah envied him his uncomplicated life and his apparently happy family. She felt relaxed and contented with him. He was as talkative as

Nicholas was sullen, as easygoing as Amanda was precise and as light-hearted as William was serious. Sarah began to spend more and more time in the stable chatting with him and less and less time in The Grange playing with her cousins.

She looked forward to seeing him every day. And her liking for him was returned a hundredfold by the stable boy, who always greeted her with great affection.

'How old are you, Jim?' she asked shyly one day, wondering if it was a rude question.

'Seventeen—eighteen come Christmas.' He nudged her and giggled. 'Too old fer ya, ent I?'

The little girl blushed.

'Don't worry—I ull wait fer ya,' he teased, roaring with laughter.

'I didn't mean...' protested Sarah hotly, then burst out laughing herself. Of course she hadn't meant anything by the question, that was obvious to both of them, but Jim found humour in every situation.

'If yer can't laugh,' he would say, 'life ent worth living.'

Jim had left school at thirteen, playing truant so often and with such steadfast determination that the authorities finally gave up on him. He could barely read or write. He neither knew nor cared anything for the world outside Croxley and his great ambition was to buy Farmer Bancroft's farm when that gentleman was too old to continue running it for himself.

He had worked for the Hamilton de Veres as a gardener and Ted Allen had inherited him, along with most of the other servants at The Grange. But it did not take the astute businessman long to discover that Jim Neeld had talents more useful to him than digging ditches or planting pansies.

'That lad is a natural with animals,' he said to his wife,

watching Jim exercising the children's new pony one morning. 'I'm so glad I gave him the job—he's the best stable boy for miles around.'

He was the best companion for Sarah too, although her uncle hadn't planned it that way. The boy had a great, round face that looked as if it had been left out in all weathers, a shock of brown hair that seemed to grow in every direction but the right one, the worst teeth Sarah had ever seen in any human head and finger nails bitten right down to the quick. But he was kind and sympathetic, ready to laugh or cry with Sarah and she felt comforted by him. In his own way, Jim Neeld soothed Sarah's troubled spirit as much as her little rabbit. And she was grateful for both of them.

They had made a small wire-fenced enclosure for Biminy in the corner of the stable and Sarah left him in it whenever she went to The Grange.

'Well, you're here most a the time,' Jim Neeld had said. 'Seems ter me ya got ter give the poor thing some place ter run. It can't spend all its time in a basket. It's cruel, ent it?'

Sarah nodded. She accepted everything Jim said about rabbits as gospel truth because the boy knew everything there was to know about them. He told Sarah about plants and trees too, about the habits of wild animals, about the movement of wind and clouds, about the problems of harvesting and the fun of beer-making.

'How do you know all that?' Sarah was a little vexed. She had been born and bred in the country too and yet it seemed to her she must have walked around all her life with her eyes and ears tightly shut.

'Me dad told me, and me grandad,' Jim explained. 'We bin country folk for generations, far back as we can

81

remember. I bet your mum and dad come up from the city, didn't they?'

'They're from London, yes. My granny and grandpa still live there.'

'There y'are then. Can't expect a poor old Londoner to know about the country, can ya?' said the stable boy, with a certain air of superiority.

'Where do you live, Jim?' asked Sarah, who thought she knew or knew of everybody living in Croxley.

'Other side a the highway—the new estate.'

'Oh.'

'Oh,' the boy echoed after her, catching exactly the note of disapproval in her voice. 'Not one a yer nobs, we ent, Sarah. Just poor folk living on a council estate.'

'Oh, Jim, I....'

''Tis all right. I know as how the Croxley people looks down on us. But we all grew too big fer the little house we used ter live in, up by Middle Farm, and when the council offered us a house me dad jumped at it. We don't like it much, mind. Me mum hates it. But it's much bigger, and cleaner, and....' He shrugged. 'You can't have everything, can ya?'

'Jim, I wasn't trying to be snobby, honestly!' protested Sarah, genuinely distressed that he had misunderstood her. 'I said "Oh" like that because one of my brother's friends—well, one of the boys he used to go around with,' she corrected herself, 'lives on the new estate. And he's horrible. It just makes me feel bad when anything reminds me of him.'

'Eddie Lewis ya mean?'

'How did you know?'

''Cause I seen um tergether—a lot.'

'Not recently?'

'Yesterday, now I comes ter think of it.'

82

'Oh no!'

'What's wrong?'

Sarah slumped against the stable door. 'He's not allowed to go out with Eddie Lewis any more. My mother warned him about it two weeks ago.'

Jim Neeld grimaced. 'She's right,' he said. 'He's a proper menace that Eddie.'

'Do you know him?'

'Know him? Everybody on the estate knows him. Allus lookin fer a fight, he is. If he don't cause somebody some trouble, he thinks he's had a bad day. He ull end up in prison right enough, you see if he don't.'

'But why is he so friendly with Nicholas? I mean....' Sarah was puzzled. 'He has a gang he goes around with, apparently, and Nicholas just isn't his type.'

'That's the point,' said Jim. 'Your brother is, well, how can I explain it to ya, he's a challenge to Eddie. He's well ter do, ent he, and Eddie Lewis is scum.'

'You mean he wants to be like Nick?' said Sarah, still confused.

'No,' Jim corrected her. 'I mean as how he wants ter pull Nick down ter his level.'

'Oh.' Sarah could find nothing else to say.

'Anyway, Eddie's got nothing better ter do with his time,' continued the stable boy. 'He's never worked— bin on the dole since he left school, he has. What he don't swindle out a the government, he steals from the rest of us on the estate.'

'Why don't the police arrest him?'

''Cause he's too sharp for um. Comes from the East End a London, he do. He leaves poor old Constable Fulton with his mouth hanging open.'

'Where did you see him with Nicholas yesterday?' said Sarah in a small voice.

'At Eddie's house, in the back yard, fiddling around with that clapped out old motor bike of his. Your brother's a real nut about motor bikes, ent he?'

Sarah said nothing. She was deep in thought, wondering whether to tell her mother about Nick's disobedience or not. But on the way home from The Grange that day, the question was answered for her.

'Oh,' said someone, as she walked down Swallow Lane in the deepening shadows of early evening. 'Oh, dear me, if it ain't Nicholas Marlowe's dear little sister.'

As soon as she heard the voice, Sarah's heart sank.

'And 'ow are we then?' Eddie Lewis sprang over the field gate and leered down at her.

The little girl recoiled, looking up at him in abject terror.

'Got our little rabbit with us, 'ave we?' he said, his voice dripping honey. Sarah put Biminy behind her back.

'Lost your tongue?' the boy jeered. 'Let me see. Let me see, I said.' He grabbed the girl before she could get away and forced open her jaws with a brutal gesture. 'Oh, it's in there all right,' he said, looking into her mouth. 'I can see it. 'Onest I can.' And he pushed her away.

Sarah landed on her back and the basket fell to one side. Before she could reach it, however, Eddie Lewis leaped forward and picked up the rabbit, clutching it to his chest.

'Give it to me!' Sarah threw herself at the boy but he raised his knee at the last moment, striking her full in the stomach. She doubled up with pain and burst into tears.

'I warned you,' said the boy, looking at her impassively. 'You got to do everythin' I say, miss, when I say it—just like that! Understand?' And he snapped his

84

fingers. 'If not....' He grasped the rabbit by the back legs and put his other hand round its neck. 'Ever seen a rabbit killed, Sarah?' His voice was soft and silky. 'You pull it out like this.' He stretched Biminy's neck and the rabbit let out a frightened squeal. 'Then, to kill it, you give it a quick twist to the right.'

Sarah flattened herself against the field gate, her eyes wide with horror.

'Just a quick twist,' said the boy, watching her reaction with interest. For an eternity he stood with the rabbit in his hands, smiling at Sarah, then he dropped it at her feet and laughed. 'Just remember, Sarah,' he said, wagging a finger at her. 'Just you remember!' He got on his motor bike and, revving the engine till it screamed, he roared away, shattering the peace of the quiet little village.

Sarah watched until he was out of sight, and even when she could no longer hear the raucous sound of the engine, she still stood there, unable to move. The rabbit lolloped over to the hedgerow and began to nibble contentedly at a stinging nettle.

'Don't ya let him eat those, Sarah. They ull upset his insides. They should be dried fust.'

It was Jim Neeld, cycling home from The Grange after his day's work. He turned to wave as he passed by. 'See ya tomorr...' he began cheerfully, then he caught sight of Sarah's face and braked sharply. 'W–what's wrong?' he said, running back to her.

She opened her mouth to speak but nothing came out except a sobbing, stifled kind of sound.

'Sarah! Sarah! What's happened then? Tell me, for Lord's sake!'

Her legs gave way and she fell against him.

'I ull get ya home, don't worry. I ull get ya home,' said

86

the boy and, stooping, he picked her up in a fireman's lift and carried her and her rabbit back to safety.

'She's had a nasty shock,' said Doctor Evans, looking at the little girl lying in bed. 'But she'll be all right. A sedative will give her a good night's rest and I suggest you keep her quiet for the next few days. No excitement of any kind.'

'Very well, doctor,' said Mrs Marlowe. 'I'll do my best.'

Sarah heard her mother go down the stairs, talking with the doctor in whispers. Nicholas stood in a corner of the bedroom, leaning against the wall, looking at his sister in a curious kind of way. He seemed uncertain how to behave.

When Mrs Marlowe came back into the room, she sat on the edge of Sarah's bed and, leaning towards her, stroked her face soothingly. 'Do you want to talk about it now, or some other time?' she said.

Sarah glanced at Nicholas over her mother's shoulder. He frowned as if he knew what was coming, but his mouth remained shut in a thin, tight line.

'It might be better if you told me now,' said Mrs Marlowe coaxingly. 'Get it off your chest, darling, and you'll feel a lot better.'

So Sarah told her mother all that had happened and by the time she had finished she was in tears again, sobbing in her mother's arms, her whole body shaking with fear and horror.

'There, there!' Mrs Marlowe rocked her back and forth as if she were a baby. 'It's all over now, sweetheart, all over. I'm going to tell the police about that wretched boy. He ought to be put away—Borstal's too good for him!'

She turned to her son. 'Now maybe you understand why I forbade you to see him again, Nick,' she said sternly. 'He's evil.'

But Nicholas turned away, his face inscrutable.

Sarah looked at him long and hard. Should she tell her mother the truth, she wondered? She felt awful carrying tales about Nicholas, especially as it would get him into trouble with his mother yet again, but wasn't that better than the terrible trouble he would surely get into with Eddie Lewis sooner or later, she reasoned? He might even end up in Borstal himself. Nick in Borstal! Her blood froze at the very thought. 'Mummy,' she blurted out. 'Mummy, Nick has been seeing Eddie Lewis. He sees him often—he even goes to his home—he was there yesterday, I know....' Her voice faded away under her brother's look of intense hatred.

Mrs Marlowe rose to her feet and stared at her son. Sarah cringed, steeling herself for the inevitable torrent of angry words, but when her mother finally spoke, her voice was amazingly controlled. 'Nicholas,' she said, 'I warned you once about seeing Eddie Lewis and it seems you have deliberately disobeyed me. I won't warn you again. If I hear you have disobeyed me a second time, I shall simply wash my hands of you altogether. I shall go to the juvenile court and I shall tell the judge I can no longer control you. You'll be put in the charge of a probation officer and you'll probably end up in an institution.' She paused. 'The choice is yours.'

Nicholas went terribly white. 'I–I...' he stammered. Then he turned and ran from the room.

Sarah could scarcely believe her ears. 'Oh Mummy,

M–M–Mummy!' she cried, quite distraught. 'You wouldn't do that to N–N–Nicholas, would you?'

Mrs Marlowe closed the door and went back to sit on her daughter's bed. 'Sarah, love,' she whispered, taking the frightened girl in her arms, 'you know I wouldn't send Nicholas away whatever happened. He's my son and I love him dearly. But I must do something to make him come to his senses before it's too late.'

'Why d'ya call it Biminy?' said Jim Neeld, looking at the rabbit as it lay dozing in the little pen in The Grange stables.

Sarah shrugged. 'Because,' she said.

The boy smiled. 'That's a good enough reason, I suppose.'

'It's a nice name for him.' Sarah put aside the tack she was cleaning and reached into the rabbit's pen. 'It's a lovely name, isn't it, old fellow?' She picked Biminy up and kissed him on the nose.

'Him?' The stable boy frowned. 'I don't think it's a him.'

'Of course it is. At least....' Sarah hesitated. She had always assumed Biminy was a male but then, she bit her lip, nobody had ever told her otherwise.

'Let me see it.' The boy held out his hands. 'I ull soon tell ya.' He lifted the rabbit's tail, and then he laughed. 'Is Biminy a girl's name too?' he said.

'Why? Oh—is he a she?'

Jim nodded. 'Oi, he is a she. And what's more, she's ready ter be mated.'

'Mated?' Sarah echoed.

'How old is she?'

'Uhm.' The girl did a rapid calculation. 'She must be about six months. Maybe a bit older.'

'Overdue,' Jim said with authority.

'But, but she c–c–can't have kittens.'

'Why not. It's cruel ter stop her. Ya should let her have one or two litters at least. Any road, you could sell um.' He ran his fingers through the rabbit's long, silky fur. 'Angoras are worth a lot.'

'But she *can't* have kittens. That's what I'm trying to tell you,' protested Sarah. 'She's crippled.'

'Sarah, Lord's sake!' Sometimes city folk exasperated Jim and he considered Sarah a city girl simply because the Marlowes hadn't lived in the country for several centuries like the Neelds. 'A crippled leg won't stop her from having kittens. Any road, t'ent that bad. Don't stop her from hopping about, do it?'

'Oh.'

He laughed. 'Don't just say "Oh".'

'But what can I do?'

'Find a buck and mate her to him.'

'But I don't know any bucks.'

'Well, now, neither do I, not personally any road. But where did ya get her from in the fust place.'

'Mrs Oliver. She's got lots of Angoras. Oh, I suppose I could mate Biminy with one of her bucks.'

'Course ya could. And if they're healthy, Mrs Oliver ull likely buy um from ya.'

Sarah's face lit up. 'What a marvellous idea,' she said, suddenly thinking of the money and all the lovely things she could buy with it. 'Do you think she will?'

'Of course I will, m'dear,' said Mrs Oliver later that evening when Sarah asked her. 'I'll give you five pounds for each kitten, providing they're healthy and strong.'

'Five pounds!' Sarah's eyes shone. 'When shall I bring Biminy to the buck, Mrs Oliver?' she said eagerly.

'You could leave her now, if you liked, love.'

But the girl looked doubtful. 'I think I'd better check with Mummy first,' she said.

Mrs Marlowe looked even more doubtful. 'It's a lot of responsibility, Sarah,' she said. 'I mean you've got to watch over Biminy carefully. It's her first litter and....'

'I'll take good care of her, Mummy, I promise.'

'And you can't keep carrying her around in that basket when she's pregnant. It will upset her.'

Sarah's heart sank. Dare she leave Biminy alone and unguarded? 'I'll risk it,' she said, her mind made up.

'Risk it?' Mrs Marlowe frowned. 'What on earth do you mean?'

'I mean I'll leave her in her hutch in the garden.'

'And what's so risky about that?'

'Oh nothing. Just a joke.' Sarah laughed it off. 'Is it all right then if I take her to Mrs Oliver's tomorrow to be mated?'

Mrs Marlowe sighed in a resigned kind of way. 'All right. Go ahead,' she said. 'It seems you're quite determined to turn this place into a rabbitry.'

'But how will I know if she's pregnant?' Sarah asked Jim

91

Neeld later that week.

''Tis very likely she is,' said the boy. 'But you ull know soon enough when she starts ter get fat and her teats fill with milk.'

'When will she have the kittens, do you think?'

'Thirty-one days from the day a mating,' said the resident rabbit authority. 'And around the twenty-fifth day, she ull start pulling the fur outa her belly to make a nest fer um.'

Sarah's heart turned over at the thought. A nest for the kittens, her kittens—seven or eight of them, Jim had said. Seven or eight tiny kittens, all soft and helpless. She could hardly wait.

Mr Oliver built a wooden nest box for them. 'Put it in her hutch 'bout a week before she kindles,' he said.

Sarah nodded wisely. Jim Neeld had already explained to her that 'kindling' was rabbit language for 'giving birth'.

'Put plenty of soft meadow hay in the box,' continued the man, who had become as much of an expert on Angoras as his wife. 'Biminy will mix it with her stomach fur to make a nice, warm bed for the babies.'

'Is there anything I should do for her in the mean-time?' said Sarah, anxious to do the right thing.

'Give her lots of drinking water, and you might add a few tasty titbits to her diet,' Mr Oliver advised, 'like carrot leaves and coltsfoot, and some brown bread baked in the oven.'

'How will I know when she's going to have the babies?'

'About twenty-four hours before she kindles, she'll go off her food completely. Don't worry about it, it's quite natural. And don't worry about her, Sarah. She's an animal. She knows how to kindle and raise her kittens without you fussing all the time.'

'Will she...?' Sarah hesitated, looking doubtfully at her rabbit. 'Will she eat her kittens if I touch them after they're born?' She could hardly bring herself to believe that dear old Biminy would do such a horrible thing, but one never knew....

'Lord, no!' The old man let out a raucous cackle. 'Whoever told you that silly old wives' tale?'

Sarah stifled a giggle. She longed to say, 'Your silly old wife,' but she kept her face quite straight and said, 'Mrs Oliver.'

'Mrs...?' His face fell. 'Oh, I see—well,' he drew Sarah towards him and whispered in her ear. 'Don't tell the missus I told you but that's all nonsense. You've handled Biminy enough for her to feel comfortable about it and she won't mind you touching her kittens either. She'd only eat them if you didn't give her enough to drink or eat, or she might get too enthusiastic about cleaning up after their birth and munch one up in mistake for the afterbirth,' he chortled, but Sarah didn't find anything funny in it.

'Hello, stranger,' said Jim Neeld the next time Sarah went to The Grange. He smiled cheerfully enough but he had a hurt, questioning look in his eyes. Sarah had scarcely been near the stables for two weeks.

'Hello, Jim.' She sat down on a stool in a corner of the stable and watched the boy brush Alexander's coat. She felt guilty about not seeing Jim Neeld and her cousins, especially as they had all been so kind to her, but she felt even guiltier about leaving Biminy by herself. The stable boy was sturdy and tough. He could take care of himself. And Amanda and William had Uncle Ted and Aunt Angela to look after them. But Biminy was a helpless little animal....

'Don't care about us no more, Alexander,' Jim said to

the horse. 'We ent important to her now.'

'Oh Jim, it isn't that. I really miss you and Alexander but....'

'Anxious mother?'

She laughed and nodded. 'Much more anxious than Biminy is. She seems quite contented.'

'You're being a bit silly, ya know,' said Jim, still looking hurt. 'She's an animal—she can take care of herself.'

'I know. I know,' Sarah cut in quickly. And she frowned. But how could she explain to the boy that she was afraid to leave Biminy alone and unprotected with her brother. It was a horrible thing to say about Nicholas, horrible even to think it. On the other hand, if something happened to the rabbit while she was away....

'And who's looking after the pregnant lady at the moment?'

'My mother.'

'Thought she went out ter work.'

'She does, usually. But she's taken two days off for a rest. She'll make sure Biminy doesn't get into any danger.'

'Danger?' The boy pounced on the word. 'What danger can a rabbit get up to in a hutch?'

'May I do that?' Sarah leaped off the stool and, grabbing the brush from the boy's hand, she started to work on the horse with great vigour. 'His coat is so beautiful, isn't it?' she said, changing the subject abruptly. 'It shines just like a....'

'Chestnut,' Jim finished the sentence for her. 'That's 'cause he is a chestnut,' he added drily. Then he leaned against a post, crossed his arms and stared at her. Sarah could feel his eyes penetrating her back, but she kept brushing furiously.

'So you're afraid as how somebody will hurt the rabbit. That's it, ent it?'

Sarah looked away, pretending not to have heard.

'Your brother, mebbe?'

She stopped, the brush in mid-air. 'N-n-no. I....'

'Aw, come on, Sarah.' The stable boy dismissed her protests with a wave of his hand. ''Tis obvious to any but a fool. Ya think yer brother's got it in fer the rabbit, don't ya?'

She nodded, her eyes on the ground. 'He's threatened several times to kill it. He's only joking...' she added hastily. Then she shook her head. 'No he isn't. He means it all right. He hates Biminy.'

'He hates everybody.'

'N-n-n-no, he doesn't.' Sarah rushed to her brother's defence. 'Nick is...oh.' She sighed. 'I don't know. He's just awful since Daddy left. Mummy doesn't know what to do with him. He won't talk to anyone. He's rude to all his old friends, especially Amanda and William. He's absolutely terrible to them.'

'Jealous,' said Jim without hesitation.

'Yes, I think so too,' Sarah agreed. 'They've got so much. Toys and games and—oh, everything they ask for they get.'

'No, I don't mean yer brother's jealous a that kind a thing.' Jim dismissed the toys and games as unimportant. 'I mean he's jealous 'cause 'Manda and Willum have a mum and dad. Ya know, a proper family....'

'Oh.' Sarah hadn't thought of that.

'I reckon that's why he and Eddie Lewis gets along so well. Eddie don't have no mum and dad, ya know. Don't know where they are even. He lives with foster parents.'

Sarah felt guilty talking to a stranger about her

brother in such a way and yet Jim wasn't a stranger. She felt closer to him than Nicholas now, closer even than her mother at times. Jim understood and cared. He had six brothers and sisters and he seemed genuinely fond of them all, but he still had love to spare for anyone who needed it.

'I ull look after Biminy,' he said after a while. 'Put her in the back garden at home.'

Sarah shook her head. 'It would look strange,' she said. 'Neither Mummy nor Nick would understand why I had done such a crazy thing.'

'Nick would. He ent no fool.'

'Anyway, you've got that awful Eddie Lewis living near you.'

The boy groaned. 'Lord, yes, I ud forgotten that dirty rat,' he said in disgust. 'But ya can't go on watching over Biminy fer ever, ya know. That'd be ridiculous. Why don't ya speak to yer brother about it. Ask him why he hates the rabbit?'

'It's no use.' Sarah stroked the soft, warm hair on Alexander's neck. 'I can't speak to Nicholas any more—about anything.'

'Then ya'll have ter get rid a Biminy.'

A look of panic sprang into the girl's eyes. Get rid of Biminy? 'Never!' she said, clenching her fists as if to ward off some unseen attacker. 'I'll never do that!'

'I don't mean put her down,' the boy explained gently. 'I just mean find another home fer her—mebbe Mrs Oliver would take her back.'

Sarah shook her head. 'I couldn't live without her now,' she whispered. 'She needs me.'

'Seems ter me...' Jim began, but he changed his mind. 'Have it yer own way,' he said, taking the brush from her and bending down to polish the horse's abdomen. 'And Sarah!' he called, as the girl walked out of the stable. 'Let me know how many kittens she has, will ya? I might buy one meself. Allus had a soft spot fer rabbits.'

As she walked down the gravel path of The Grange, Sarah suddenly had a marvellous idea. She would give Jim a kitten, the best of the litter. She smiled to herself and did a little skip and jump, imagining the boy's surprised face when she presented him with the baby rabbit. She would put it in a basket, no, a box, with a big bow on the top, just for fun, and when he opened it....

But the happy thoughts vanished when Sarah got home. Her mother greeted her with a gloomy face.

'What's wrong?' said Sarah alarmed.

Mrs Marlowe slumped down at the kitchen table and sank her head in her hands. 'Constable Fulton was here a few moments ago.'

Sarah felt the sinking feeling in her stomach that was becoming all too familiar. 'W-w-why?' she whispered.

'Dick Morris—the landlord at the Rose and Crown— he bought some dogs, Doberman pinschers, to protect himself,' Mrs Marlowe said in a lifeless voice. 'Do you remember?'

Sarah nodded.

'They're both dead,' continued her mother without looking up. 'Somebody stabbed them—last night. Dick found them this morning when he went to their kennel....' Her voice faded away.

'Oh no!'

'Beautiful dogs,' her mother murmured, as if in a dream, 'so strong....'

'And C-C-Constable Fulton thinks that Nicholas...?'

'He suspects him,' said Mrs Marlowe. 'There's no

definite proof but Nicholas was seen last night near the Rose and Crown.'

Sarah's knees buckled and she sat down. 'But Nicholas was here last night. He was asleep in b-b-bed,' she protested.

'How do you know?'

'Well, he always is—isn't he?' Sarah finished lamely, realizing how futile her protest was. 'What does Nicholas say?'

'I haven't seen him since breakfast. He's very wisely keeping out of my way. Constable Fulton is looking for him too.'

'What will they do to him when they find him, Mummy? Will he be arrested?'

'I don't know, darling. I just don't know. They may....' She lapsed into silence.

'They may—what?' thought Sarah. 'Send Nick away?' That was too terrible even to think about.

Nicholas came home in the early evening and went straight up to his room.

'Nick!' his mother called him.

'Yes?' he paused, halfway up the stairs.

Mrs Marlowe went to the living room door. 'Do you know...?' she said. 'Have you...?' But she couldn't bring herself to complete the question.

'Dick Morris's dogs are dead,' said the boy in a flat voice.

His mother nodded.

'I suppose I did that as well?' he said.

'Nick, I didn't say....' His mother made to follow him but he had gone, slamming his bedroom door behind him.

'Nick wouldn't do such a thing,' protested Sarah when Mrs Marlowe came back into the living room, looking quite defeated. 'He loves animals. He wouldn't harm....' And then she suddenly remembered Biminy.

Constable Fulton came to the house the next morning. As soon as he arrived, Mrs Marlowe took him and her son into the living room and closed the door. Sarah escaped to the garden and busied herself cleaning out the rabbit's hutch but she could still hear angry voices from inside the house, however hard she tried to blot them out.

After twenty minutes or so, the policeman left. Nicholas went out shortly after. Sarah saw him leave the house, hands in his pockets, shoulders hunched over, eyes fixed on the ground, the very picture of defiant misery.

Sarah put Biminy back into the hutch. The doe was swelling noticeably now and Sarah handled her with care, then she crept into the kitchen, almost afraid to learn the outcome of Constable Fulton's visit. She had a horror of Nick being led away in handcuffs, but it hadn't come to that, thank goodness.

Mrs Marlowe was washing up the breakfast dishes, attacking plates and pots with such fury Sarah was surprised they didn't crack. She turned and saw her daughter standing hesitantly by the door, a questioning look on her troubled face.

'It's all right,' she said tersely. 'He gave Nick another warning. They can't prove he did it. On the other hand

100

Nick can't prove that he didn't.'

'Where was Nick last night, Mummy? Was he near the Rose and Crown. D–d–did he say?' Sarah asked.

'He wouldn't. Constable Fulton asked him over and over again and all he'd say in that sullen way of his was, "I felt like going for a walk. It's a free world, isn't it? I can go for a walk if I feel like it."'

Mrs Marlowe attacked a pot with a scouring pad, scrubbing and scrubbing as if she were cleaning out the inside of her son's insolent mouth. 'I've never heard Nick speak so rudely to anyone. I tried to make him apologize but he wouldn't. You know, Sarah'—she stopped what she was doing and her whole body seemed to sag under the weight of her troubles—'sometimes I think Nick does his level best to antagonize everybody, especially me. He keeps pushing and pushing—and I just can't take it any more.'

She put a hand over her eyes and bent her head. 'I simply can't take it any more,' she said in a strangled voice.

Terrified, Sarah ran out of the house and up Swallow Lane. Her whole world was crashing around her. Even her mother couldn't cope.

'Hey there, steady on!' A man laughed as Sarah ran headlong into him. 'What are you trying to do, knock me for six?'

Sarah looked up.

'Oh, Uncle Ted. I—I....'

'What's wrong, love?' He bent down and put his hands on her shoulders. 'What's happened this time?'

'It's M–Mummy,' she cried. 'I think she's going to l–l–leave us too!'

And, burying her face in the soft wool of her uncle's sweater, she sobbed her heart out.

101

School started again at the beginning of September. Sarah tossed and turned sleeplessly, the way she always did the night before the first day back. To make it worse, she was uneasy about having to leave Biminy by herself all day, even though Nicholas would be at school too. The doe was heavily pregnant, her kittens due at any moment, and the slightest upset might make her miscarry.

Sarah's heart sank at the thought. For the few hours that she did sleep, she dreamed deliriously of Eddie Lewis, his hands about Biminy's neck, twisting, twisting.... Nick's face floated ominously through her dreams too, and she woke at dawn in a cold sweat of horror and fear.

It was a dull, grey day, and by the time Sarah got wearily out of bed, it had started to rain.

'Eat a good breakfast,' her mother advised, putting a plate of scrambled eggs in front of her. 'You too, Nick. You need plenty of energy for school. You've got used to the soft life, you know.' She smiled wryly. 'It's back to work for both of you today.'

Sarah shook her head and pushed the plate away. 'I'm not hungry,' she mumbled.

Her mother clucked disapproval. 'Darling, it's only first day nerves. You'll feel better when you get there. You know you always do.'

Nicholas also pushed his plate away and rose to leave.

'And where do you think you're going?' demanded his mother acidly, eyeing his retreating back. 'Sit down and finish your food, please.'

'I thought I'd go and spend the day up on Wright's Farm,' Nicholas said, with determined casualness, and he headed towards the door, ignoring his mother's request to sit down again at the breakfast table.

'You thought you'd what?' Mrs Marlowe could hardly believe her ears.

'I'm not going to school.' Nick was quite matter of fact about it. 'I think it's a stupid waste of time. I'm going to get a job on a farm. Earn some money of my own—then I'll be free.'

He turned and looked at his mother, a cold, hard expression on his face, almost as if he were willing her to contradict him.

For a moment Mrs Marlowe was speechless. She looked at her son, astounded, and he glared back at her, waiting.

Sarah was even more perturbed. She had banked on her brother being at school all day, not roaming the countryside looking for mischief.

'May I be excused?' she said. And without waiting for an answer, she leaped to her feet and went to the door.

Mrs Marlowe, suddenly distracted from her rebellious son, shouted after her, 'Clean socks, Sarah. And don't forget to polish your shoes as well.'

The girl raced upstairs, dressed rapidly, ignoring the instruction about her shoes, threw on her blazer and hat, grabbed her satchel and raced down again, out into the garden. She opened the rabbit's hutch, and, lifting Biminy as gently as she could, she placed her in the basket.

'Sarah!'

Her mother's voice made her jump and she nearly dropped the rabbit.

'Why are you wasting time with that rabbit? You should be on your way to school by now!'

The girl picked up the basket and turned to face her mother. She was standing by the open window, hands on hips, eyes blazing. Sarah had never seen her so angry. Nicholas hovered in the background. Obviously the heated argument between the two had been momentarily interrupted.

'I'm going to take Biminy to....' Sarah stopped herself just in time. She had been about to say that she was taking the rabbit to the safety of Jim Neeld's stable, but that would have been stupid. 'I'm going to take her to school with me,' she said.

'To school? What utter nonsense!' her mother exploded. 'She's going to have her kittens in a day or so. Put her back in the hutch this minute!'

'But Mummy....'

'Enough!' Mrs Marlowe shouted, striking the window pane with her fist. 'Do as I tell you!'

Tearfully Sarah put Biminy back in the hutch, stroked her gently and, without another word, walked towards the gate.

'And as for you, Nicholas...' said Mrs Marlowe, turning her attention back to her son.

'I told you I'm not going to school today or tomorrow or ever. And you can't make me!' yelled the boy.

'We'll see about that!'

Sarah walked out into the lane, her heart heavy. Nicholas wouldn't go to school. Once he had made up his mind, nothing could budge him. But his mother had to go to work. There were people away sick and she was desperately needed. That meant that Biminy would be alone all day.

'Hello, Sarah,' a voice called cheerfully as she passed

The Grange.

Sarah jumped and, turning, saw Amanda coming down the path towards her.

'I suppose you didn't recognize me,' said Amanda slyly.

'Didn't rec....' Sarah frowned and then, realizing what her cousin meant, she blushed. 'I'm terribly sorry, Amanda,' she said, trying to look contrite. 'I know I haven't been to see you much lately, but you see....'

'Yes, yes, I know,' the other girl interrupted, 'Biminy's going to have babies. Everybody knows. The whole village knows,' and she laughed. 'Are you going to school now?'

Sarah nodded. 'First day.'

'I start on Wednesday.' Amanda pulled a face. 'Wish I didn't.'

'Don't you like it?'

'Oh, it's all right. But I'd rather stay here all the time, wouldn't you?'

Sarah didn't answer. Home was no longer the place she wanted to be.

'Amanda, will you do me a big favour?' she said suddenly, clutching at her cousin's arm.

Amanda winced at the strength of Sarah's grip. 'What?' she said, taken aback by her cousin's intensity.

'Will you g-g-go to my home and get Biminy and bring her back here for the day. I'll collect her on my way home this evening. Be very careful with her though, because she's....'

But Amanda was already shaking her head. 'I'm going out with Mummy,' she said. 'We've got to buy some boring stuff like socks and shoes and things....'

A car rolled slowly down the drive towards them.

'Here comes Mummy now,' said Amanda. 'Sorry,

105

Sarah. I could do it tomorrow for you....'

Sarah's face fell.

'Good morning,' Aunt Angela called. 'Can we give you a lift to school, darling?'

'No thanks.' Sarah's school was a mile or so from her home. 'I like to walk,' she added.

'Well, come on, Amanda,' urged her mother. 'Don't just stand there, dear. You know I want to get going. I have to be back by twelve for the Women's Institute lunch.'

'Sarah!' Amanda called after her cousin, who was almost out of earshot.

'What?'

'Will you save one of Biminy's kittens for me? Daddy says he'll buy me one.'

'O.K.' Sarah tried to smile. One for Amanda and one for Jim Neeld, she thought, trudging through the drizzling rain. That is, if there are any kittens at all.

When Sarah got to school she was greeted by a group of her old friends, all of whom were talking excitedly about the long summer holidays and all that had happened. For a while Sarah tried to chat and laugh with them but she could no longer join in. Outside school their worlds were now quite separate and, indeed, as Sarah's thoughts turned homewards again, she became withdrawn and silent. The other girls stole quick glances at her when she wasn't looking, then they turned to each other and raised their eyebrows or shrugged.

All through the morning Sarah's thoughts centred on the defenceless rabbit and several times she was brought back to the present with an angry, 'Sarah, for goodness' sake concentrate!' from Mrs Prince.

She was desperate to see Biminy, to know the little animal was safe. But how could she get away?

At the beginning of the lunch break, she approached her teacher hesitantly. 'May I go home, please?' she said, in what she hoped was a very sick voice. 'I don't feel well.'

'What's wrong, dear?' Mrs Prince was a kindly soul behind the rather severe exterior.

'I've....' Sarah thought rapidly. 'I've got a stomach ache.'

The woman looked at her closely. 'Something's wrong, isn't it, Sarah? Something's worrying you. Do you want to talk about it?'

'No, oh no. Nothing's wrong. Everything's just f-f-fine.' Sarah bit her lip. She had sounded far too emphatic and she wished she hadn't stammered at that moment.

Mrs Prince laid a hand on her shoulder. 'I think you're just suffering from nerves, dear,' she said sympathetically. 'Go and lie down in Nurse William's room for half an hour. I'll bring you a glass of hot milk.'

Sarah winced. That was not what she wanted to do. And hot milk was worse than poison.

'And Sarah...' Mrs Prince called after her as she dragged herself away, 'if you want to talk about—well, anything, any problems—you know I'm always here. And I'm very good at keeping secrets.'

Sarah turned and smiled. But she said nothing.

The nurse was away, presumably at lunch, so Sarah crawled on to the bunk, covered herself with the red scratchy blanket and closed her eyes. She had meant to lie there for the prescribed time and then rejoin her friends in the playground, but when Mrs Prince crept in, half an hour later, the girl was fast asleep, her face set in an anxious frown, her fists clenched tightly on the red blanket.

The woman looked at her for a while, then she shook her head and went away, closing the door very quietly behind her.

Sarah never slept during the day, except when she was ill, but she was tired after her bad night and worn down by anxiety. She lay on the bunk for a long time, sleeping restlessly and occasionally uttering little whimpers of distress. Inevitably, the hated face of Eddie Lewis crept back into her dreams. The boy was stroking Biminy, running his hand up and down her back in an affectionate way, but every time his hand reached her neck, he squeezed, a little harder every time, until the rabbit was gasping for breath. Suddenly Nicholas appeared and, grabbing the rabbit by its crippled leg, he swung it round and round his head, faster and faster and faster.

'Nick, no!' Sarah screamed, sitting bolt upright. She looked around her, frightened, confused. Then she slowly realized where she was. Swinging her legs over the edge of the bunk, she sat for a while, uncertain what to do.

She glanced at her watch. Half past two! Her class would be halfway through the first lesson of the afternoon by now. But where was her class and what was the first lesson? What was the second, for that matter? She had left her satchel and books in Room 2B, she couldn't go in and interrupt them in the middle of a lesson.

The timetable for the term was new and Sarah couldn't remember what subjects were scheduled for Monday afternoons. Geography, was it? Or Biology? She racked her brains. No, something nice, something fun—netball. Yes, that was it.

She glanced at her watch again. Twenty to three. Just another fifty minutes before the final bell. Surely if she

108

went home now, nobody would miss her. After all, it was only netball, not a proper lesson.

Having given her conscience all kinds of rational reasons for playing truant, Sarah finally slipped off the bunk, folded the blanket neatly and left it on a chair, opened the door and, checking that nobody was in sight, tiptoed down the corridor to the main door.

She could hear children and teachers in classrooms as she passed but the main hall was deserted. If she could only get to the door without being seen or heard. If only.... As she turned the handle a group of children in the music room suddenly burst into song, accompanied by a shrill piano.

'John Brown's body lies a-mould'ring in the grave,' they bellowed. 'John Brown's body lies a mould-'ring....' Sarah's heart leaped. Nobody would hear her now. She opened the door and flew out of the school, down the main street, past the village store and along Swallow Lane.

She ran all the way, not even stopping to greet Mr Haines, the beagle man, who grunted, 'Danged Marlowes. No manners!' as she raced by. Nor did she give a second glance to Mrs Oliver, who followed the girl's receding back with a look of hurt amazement.

'Well, I never!' she exclaimed in disgust.

But Sarah was oblivious to all their comments. 'I'm coming, Biminy,' she cried, repeating it over and over. 'I'm coming!'

Ignoring the door of her house, she ran down the side path to the garden gate, threw it open and hurled herself across the grass to the hutch in the far corner.

It was empty.

Sarah knelt down, trembling, and opened it. She felt inside, under the hay, in every corner. Even the nest box

109

had gone.

The world turned upside down quite violently and she grabbed at the hutch for support, falling to her knees.

Biminy had gone! Biminy had gone! Her heart pounded out the refrain. Somebody had taken her, killed her! Who? Nicholas! No, no, oh please God, no!

She had to get help. Jim Neeld would help her. He would tell her what to do. He would find the rabbit. He would....

Sobbing, she ran out of the garden and back up Swallow Lane. She arrived at The Grange breathless, her face bright red from the effort, her heart pounding. As she ran down the drive towards the stable, she shouted at the top of her voice, 'Jim! Jim!'

But the stable was empty. Only Alexander watched her with great enquiring eyes as she rushed from stall to stall screaming, 'Jim! Jim! Oh please, Jim, be here! Please be here!' But no voice answered hers.

Gradually her screams faded to a whimper and she knelt down in the hay, burying her face in its prickly comfort, and wept. Alexander stamped impatiently and pulled at his block. Sarah usually brought him a carrot or a piece of sugar or something equally nice. Today she had rushed in like a whirlwind, screaming hysterically, and had ignored him altogether. He neighed irritably and stamped again.

The girl looked up, startled. It was almost as if she had forgotten the pony, but now she looked at him keenly, an idea forming in her mind. Pulling herself slowly to her feet as if the effort pained her, she brushed the tears from her face and went over to the wall where a handsome pigskin saddle was hanging. She took it down and put it on Alexander's back, strapping it in place. Then she put on his bridle and, leading him out of the stable, she sprang lightly on to his back.

'Come on, Alexander,' she said, leaning forward to whisper in his ear as if they were both part of a conspiracy. 'Come on, old fellow. You and I are going away. A long long way from here. As far as we can!' She spurred him forward and the chestnut, always eager for exercise, set off at a gallop, down the path to the great iron gates.

'Good after…' began Tom, the gardener, as the girl swept by, but she didn't notice him. Wild-eyed, white-faced, she noticed nothing. Nor cared.

Sarah's aunt, seeing her ride out on to the road, opened the window and shouted after her, 'Come back, Sarah. You know you're not allowed to….'

But the girl had gone, through the gates and up Swallow Lane, the pony going like the wind, his ears pinned back, his eyes wide with excitement and pleasure.

'We're going away!' cried the girl on his back, urging him to go faster, faster. 'We're going away!' she cried. 'And we're never coming back!'

Sarah didn't know how long she rode on the back of the handsome chestnut. Time no longer mattered to her. Nothing mattered. She let the pony have his head and he galloped flat out across fields, over hedges and ditches, through wooded glades, past tiny cottages and great manor houses. Sarah was not aware of the world

flashing past her nor did she care that, when Alexander took a gate too fast or thundered through a forest of low-hanging branches, she was in great danger of being thrown.

'Runaway horse! Runaway horse!' shrieked a woman as it hurtled by.

'Hey! Hey! What the devil d'ya think ya're up to?' shouted a farmer as Alexander galloped full tilt through a field of precious crops. But Sarah barely heard him.

At last the chestnut slowed to a halt. He was sweating heavily and his withers twitched with the strain of the ride. Wearily Sarah dismounted and looked about her. She was in another stable, bigger than the one at The Grange. Other horses were there too, tethered in their stalls, and they neighed at Alexander as if in greeting.

'I suppose this is your old home,' she said to the sweating horse. 'That's why you brought me here, wasn't it?' She stroked his neck and put her arms about him, leaning against him for a while, her eyes closed. She remembered how Jim Neeld had told her the pony came from a big stable in Kidderton.

'I takes him back thur sometimes—just ter see all his old mates,' Jim had said. 'Loves it, he do.'

Kidderton, Sarah frowned, that was a long way from Croxley. A long way—but not far enough.

'You must go back now, old fellow,' she said. 'You must go home—or they'll follow me here.' And, leading Alexander to the stable entrance, she whacked him sharply on the rump. With a startled neigh, he reared and cantered around the yard, tossing his head uneasily as if he were unsure what to do. But Sarah ran at him, clapping her hands and shouting, and with another loud neigh, the pony suddenly turned and galloped off in the direction he had come.

Sarah went back into the stable and looked around her with unseeing eyes. Later she would go, she told herself. Later she would run away, maybe take another horse and ride on, as far as she could to get away from home. But for now, she sank down into a pile of hay in a corner of the stable and curled into a little ball.

What had Nicholas done with the rabbit, she wondered? Had he hidden her, killed her? Almost certainly he had killed her, he and that wretched, loathsome Eddie Lewis. And the kittens? All dead too. Every tiny, helpless, fragile body. She would never forgive Nicholas. She would never see him again as long as she lived. Never.

Sarah woke in the late evening to the sound of voices. She sat up with a start and uttered a little cry of fear. It was cold and dark and she didn't know where she was. The voices were close by, and familiar. Yet, in her groggy, befuddled state, she couldn't place them. A horse stamped nearby and suddenly she remembered the mad gallop on Alexander's back. And those voices—wasn't that Uncle Ted? He was talking to someone. But who?

Getting stiffy to her feet, Sarah crept to the stable door and looked out. It was a moonless night and the yard was dark but the farmhouse door stood open and in its light Sarah saw Uncle Ted and another man. There was also a boy standing next to Uncle Ted. It was.... Sarah's heart did a great leap—it was Nicholas!

She cowered back into the darkness, straining to listen. Snatches of their conversation came to her.

'...just before supper....' It was the man speaking.

'...girl riding it?' Uncle Ted. He sounded strained, anxious, not at all like the easygoing man she knew.

'...only saw the horse galloping away.'

'...must be here, somewhere.' Uncle Ted.

'Let's look...torch....' Nicholas was speaking now. He sounded excited.

'Give you a hand...search...start with the stable...' said the strange man.

Fearfully Sarah crept back into the darkest corner of the stable, feeling her way lest she bump into something. A rough, hairy thing brushed her face and she let out a little scream, recoiling in horror. Spiders' webs, she thought, shuddering. Then she realized it was much too substantial for a web and, reaching up, discovered an old horse blanket thrown casually over a beam. Hastily she pulled it down and covered her body with it, scrunching herself as tightly into the corner as she could so that the blanket would look as if it had been thrown there.

The voices were getting closer now and much clearer.

'Let's start here, anyway,' said the man. 'If she's not here, we'll look in the granary and the cowsheds, then down along the river bank. There are plenty of good places to hide there. I know. My kids do it all the time, specially when there's work to be done.'

Lights flashed.

'Sarah! Sarah!' shouted Uncle Ted, so close she could almost have reached out and touched his leg.

'Sarah. Oh come on!' cried Nick.

The girl squeezed her eyes tightly shut and stopped

breathing. The smell of the horse blanket was sickening but it was better than being discovered by her uncle and wretched brother. Anything was better than that. The nerve of Nicholas coming to look for her. The nerve! She'd rather die than go back with him.

'Sarah!' Uncle Ted was pleading.

'Let's try the granary,' said the other man after a while. 'There's lots of hay there. It's the kind of place I'd hide if I were a kid.'

'You may be right....' Her uncle sounded so worried, so dejected, and Sarah suffered her first pang of guilt.

'Have you called the police?'

'Not yet,' said Uncle Ted. 'We were going to but when we got your phone call, we decided we'd come out here first.'

'Best to get the police in, you know, just in case,' said the man.

'I know. But her mother's very upset. There's been quite a lot of trouble in the family lately. Her brother's been mixed up with the wrong boys....'

'Ah, I see....'

The voices receded gradually as the men walked away.

'Lucky the horse came back here,' said the man. 'They have an incredible homing instinct.'

'Yes, but Sarah....'

'...could be miles away by now,' agreed the man.

'....don't find her soon....' They were moving out of Sarah's hearing again. '...call the police....' Uncle Ted was saying.

'...best thing,' agreed the farmer. '...never know ...all kinds of danger...especially at night...should be soundly punished...deserves it...great worry....'

When she was quite sure they had gone, Sarah

116

pushed the smelly blanket aside and sat up, leaning on one elbow. She felt very badly about her mother. It was true that the woman had suffered enough with Nick's foolishness and now she was adding to her mother's misery. But how could she go back and live with Nicholas again knowing he had killed her rabbit, destroyed the creature she loved most dearly? He was a monster, a devil! She clenched her fists in a spasm of rage. She never wanted to see him again! Besides, she suddenly thought, her heart sinking, what would happen to her if they did find her? Her mother would be furious, Uncle Ted would never speak to her again, nobody would. She might even be sent away. They were going to call in the police, after all.

It was best to move on, she decided, best to keep running so they would never find her. She would send a letter to her mother later. Her mother would understand. Wouldn't she?

Sarah's courage and determination were fading fast. The stable was dark and cold and she suddenly felt very alone, very small and vulnerable....

'Sarah!' A voice whispered close to her ear.

The girl nearly jumped out of her skin.

'Sarah!' It was Nicholas.

She held her breath.

'I know you're there,' breathed her brother. 'You were hiding under the blanket in the corner. Uncle Ted didn't see you but I saw a piece of your coat sticking out.' He giggled, a nervous giggle, as if he hoped she would laugh too. But only a stony silence greeted him.

'Sarah?' he said again, after a long pause. Then, rather gingerly, he reached out and touched the blanket, feeling for her body underneath it. His fingers brushed her arm.

117

'Leave me alone!' she lashed out at him, furious that he had touched her. 'Go away! G-g-go away! I hate you! I . . . .'

'Biminy's all right, Sarah,' Nicholas cut in quickly. 'Jim Neeld's got her. He had her all the time.'

At first she didn't understand what her brother had said. Biminy's all right? She was so sure the rabbit was dead she found it difficult, impossible to believe anything else. It was as if she didn't want to believe anything else. Her mind had accepted the death of the rabbit, terrible as it was. And then the truth hit her like a shock wave. Biminy's all right! Biminy's all right! Sarah felt joy flood through her whole being.

'Alive!' she repeated in a daze.

'You didn't really think that I'd—that I'd hurt her, did you?'

Sarah barely heard her brother. She was lost in a happy reverie.

'Did you?' he repeated.

'Well, you killed Dick Morris's dogs,' she said, some of the happy glow beginning to wear off.

'I did not!'

'Yes you did!' Sarah warmed to the attack. 'You were seen, late at night . . . .'

'I only wanted to talk to Eddie without Mum knowing.'

'As usual,' Sarah sneered.

'I mean I had to tell him I couldn't see him again and to stop bugging me. I knew he'd be hanging around the Rose and Crown with the other guys—he enjoys annoying Dick Morris—so I went up there to talk to him and . . . .'

'Oh come on, Nick!' Sarah turned away in disgust. The very thought of Eddie Lewis filled her with revulsion and she was quite sure her brother was lying anyway.

'At least have the guts to admit....'

'It's true, Sarah,' he protested. 'He'd been on at me for weeks and weeks to'—Nicholas hesitated—'to—well, he was pretty rotten,' he finished, changing his mind.

'To what?' Sarah persisted, intrigued.

'He wanted me to go out with him and the others to, oh, you know, steal things, break into people's houses when they're out.'

'Nick!' Sarah was aghast.

'He's already done it, several times, a couple of houses in Bodington. He got some silver and stuff.'

'And did you...?'

Nicholas ignored the question. 'I told him to lay off,' he said. 'I'd had enough with the police and Mum on my back all the time. But he got nasty. He said he'd—he'd fix me.'

'What did he mean fix you?' Sarah was mystified.

'He killed the dogs. Everybody thought I'd done it....'

Sarah was horrified, then relieved. It wasn't Nick. Thank God, it wasn't Nick after all.

'What a swine he is,' she said, clenching her fists so tightly she drove her nails into the flesh. 'I'd like to—I'd like to....'

'Don't worry, he's gone away. His parents have kicked him out.'

'His foster parents, you mean?'

'How did you know that? Who told you?' Sarah felt her brother looking at her, though she couldn't see him.

'Good riddance to bad rubbish,' she said, ignoring his question. 'Where's he gone?'

'Back to London.'

'I hope the police catch him,' she spat out her hatred. Nicholas said nothing. The two children sat in the

119

corner of the stable in total darkness. Nicholas had a torch in his hand but he didn't turn it on. It was as if the things they had to say to each other were best said under the cover of night.

'How's Biminy?' said Sarah, after a long pause.

'Fine. Jim said not to worry about her. She's safe with him.'

Sarah felt a great rush of gratitude to the stable boy. 'Why has he got her?'

'He saw Eddie hanging around our house at lunch time and we weren't home so he decided Biminy would be safe with him. He was right,' added the boy ruefully, 'Eddie was longing to get at her. Then everyone would have blamed me again.'

Sarah felt very guilty. She had been wrong about Nicholas on every count. She had let him down.

'You went to school then?'

'Course I did!' A resentful note was creeping back into his voice. It was the first time Sarah had spoken to her brother for many months, ever since their father had left home. There were so many questions she wanted to ask him, so many things to talk about, but she was afraid to start in case he went back into his shell.

'Sarah.' Nick's voice sounded very small in the great, dark stable.

'Yes?'

'I'm—I'm sorry—about Biminy. I—I didn't mean....' He seemed to drag the words out one by one.

'It's all right,' she said quickly.

'We didn't know where you'd gone. We looked everywhere. We—Mum....' He choked.

'Is she very upset?' Sarah asked in a small voice.

'She cried. She cried a lot. She kept saying it was all her fault.'

Sarah felt the tears welling up in her eyes. She put a hand to her lips to stop them quivering. 'I'm sorry,' she whispered.

Again she felt her brother looking at her in the inky blackness. 'You're coming back home now, aren't you?' he said as if her weren't sure of her answer.

Sarah nodded, fighting back the tears.

'Sarah?' It was a cry of anguish. 'I said are you coming home...?'

'Yes, yes, Nick, I am,' she said, frightened by her brother's intensity. 'It was silly of me. When I couldn't find Biminy, I thought she—I thought you....'

Again they sat in silence, Sarah thinking about the day, the long, long day she had just lived through. 'Nick?' she said after a while, summoning up her courage.

'What?'

She felt him turn towards her.

'You're—you're really....' She didn't know how to put the question without upsetting her brother. 'You feel really bad—about Daddy leaving, don't you?' she said. 'I mean—really bad?' she repeated, treading very carefully, dreading his reaction.

Nicholas said nothing.

Sarah's heart sank. She had made him angry again, she had turned him away. But when Nicholas finally spoke, Sarah knew he had been crying.

'Why did he—do it?' he said in a strangled voice.

'Because he wasn't happy. Mummy wasn't happy either. They just didn't want to live together any more....' Sarah, relieved, let the words flow out of her in a great torrent. 'But he still l-l-loves us, Nick. He still loves you.'

'But why did he go away? I mean—why so far away?'

'Because he had to. It's his work. He has to go wherever they want him to, doesn't he?'

'He could write.'

'He's very busy.'

'He could write!' Nicholas shouted angrily.

Sarah faltered. She realized she was saying all the right things, all the things Mummy and Uncle Ted and Aunt Angela said to reassure her—but she was not saying what she truly felt.

'We'll never see him again, will we, Nick?' she said in a small, lost voice.

Her brother mumbled something incoherent.

'He's never c–c–coming back again, is he?' she whispered, saying out loud the things she had secretly dreaded for so long. 'He doesn't care about us any more. He doesn't want us. We'll never see him again....'

Nicholas cried again. And Sarah, who thought she had no more tears left to weep, wept with him.

After a while she felt very cold and shivery and, reaching out her hand, she touched her brother's. 'Nick—I'm sorry—about Biminy,' she gulped. 'I did think—because you were so awful—but....'

'Are you coming home now?'

'Yes.'

'O.K.,' he muttered. And, taking her hand, he held it tightly, so tightly she thought he would never let it go.

Uncle Ted drove them home.

122

He spoke no word of reproach to Sarah and, though it was almost midnight when they got back to Croxley, neither did her mother. She simply took the girl in her arms and hugged her, rocking her back and forth as if she were a little baby again.

'I'm sorry,' said Sarah, looking guiltily at her mother's tear-stained face. 'I'm really sorry....' But Mrs Marlowe put a finger on her daughter's mouth.

'I was to blame too,' she whispered. 'Let's forget it, darling.'

'Is Biminy...?' began Sarah.

'Biminy is perfectly all right,' said her mother. 'Safely tucked up with Alexander in the stable.'

'We're all taking turns watching over her,' said Uncle Ted, smiling for the first time. 'Come and visit her in the morning, sweetheart.'

'O.K.,' Sarah agreed. She really was too weary to go up to The Grange that night—almost too weary to drag herself up the stairs to bed.

Bed. How lovely it was to be home in her own bed after the cold, dark loneliness of that stable. And how lovely to know that she and Nicholas were friends again, after so long, and Biminy was safe and her mother had forgiven her and—her eyes closed and she slept, a long, dreamless sleep.

When she finally woke the sun was well up and the morning almost over. Sarah leaped out of bed and, pulling on a dressing gown, she ran downstairs. Her mother was sitting at the kitchen table, drinking a cup of coffee, Nicholas beside her. The breakfast dishes hadn't been cleared away and Sarah knew, without being told, that her mother and brother had been having a long, long talk.

But Sarah had other things on her mind.

'Mummy,' she cried, 'it's a quarter past eleven. Why didn't you wake me earlier?'

'We tried,' Nick teased. 'We hit you with a crowbar several times, but you didn't move.'

'You were sleeping so soundly it seemed a pity,' said her mother. 'Have a bite to eat, love, then you can go and see Biminy.'

'Do I have to go to school this afternoon?' said Sarah doubtfully.

Mrs Marlowe shook her head, smiling. 'I think we could all do with a day off, don't you?'

Sarah bolted down a slice of toast and a glass of milk, then, dressing with the speed of greased lightning, she dashed out of the house and along Swallow Lane to The Grange.

Jim Neeld met her at the door of the stable but, before she could say anything, he raised a cautionary finger to his lips. 'Easy! Easy!' he rebuked her, a wicked smile on his face. 'Ya don't rush into a maternity ward like a bull in a china shop, do ya?'

'A materni...! Oh, Jim, really?'

Sarah tiptoed over to the pen. Biminy was lying contentedly in one corner.

'Look in thur, then,' said Jim. And, peering into the nest box, Sarah let out a gasp of delight.

'She's had them! She's had her kittens!' she cried. 'Oh, Jim, she's had her kittens!' And, grabbing the boy by the shoulders, she reached up and kissed him enthusiastically on the cheek.

'Yer, hold on,' he laughed, embarrassed yet pleased. 'I didn't have anything ter do with it, ya know. She done it all by herself.'

'How many are there?' Sarah looked into the nest again, trying to count the heap of naked kittens.

'Six.'

'Six! How marvellous! Are they all...?' she hesitated.

'All sound a wind and healthy a limb,' Jim smiled. 'I already checked um.'

Sarah reached over and stroked Biminy gently. 'Dear old girl,' she said. And then a thought occurred to her. 'Was she here—all the time?' she said. 'I mean—was she here yesterday afternoon?'

Jim nodded. 'Oi. I put a note in ya letter box telling ya as how I ud taken the rabbit and she were safe with me up at The Grange.'

'I didn't g–g–go into the house,' Sarah said, feeling rather silly about the whole thing.

'Well, I don't understand why ya didn't see her when ya come up. She were in her pen, same as allus.' He paused and rubbed his chin thoughtfully. 'Course, she mighta bin in the nest box, now I comes ter think on it, 'cause she did have the kittens some time during the night.' He paused again, then added quietly, 'Ya didn't ought ter run away like that, Sarah. Yer uncle were real worried, and as fer yer Mum and Nick....'

Sarah blushed and looked away. 'I know,' she mumbled. She got to her feet and reached into the box to stroke Biminy.

The boy looked at her anxiously. 'Ya're not thinking a moving her, are ya?' he said. 'She should stay yer fer a few more days.'

'Don't worry,' Sarah reassured him. 'I was just giving her one last stroke before I go and get Mummy and Nick. Have Amanda and William seen the kittens yet, Jim?'

'Ya're kidding. They was yer all morning. Can't keep um away,' the boy laughed. 'Specially 'Manda. She's heartbroken about leaving um tomorrow. She's got ter go ter school, ya know. Boarding school.' He made a face. 'Even your aunt and uncle was yer ter have a look at um.'

'Uncle Ted?' Sarah frowned. 'Didn't he go to work today?'

Jim shook his head. 'He looks all in,' he said. 'Reckon ya tired him out last night, gallivanting all over the countryside like that.'

'I'm going to fetch Mummy and Nicholas now,' said Sarah, anxious to change the subject. 'I'll be right back.'

She skipped down Swallow Lane towards her home, so lighthearted she felt like a leaf fluttering in the breeze. She would give a kitten to Jim and one to Amanda and one to William and one to Nicholas, if he wanted it, and—oh well, she giggled to herself, there would be hardly any left to sell to Mrs Oliver at that rate. But what did it matter? Biminy would have more kittens—lots more.

'Sarah!'

'What?' She had been so engrossed with her own happy thoughts she had not noticed the big Daimler drawn up at the kerb.

'Get in, darling.' It was Uncle Ted, beaming like a Cheshire cat.

'Why? W–w–where are we going?'

Her uncle held the door open. Nicholas was in the back seat, looking very excited.

'Where are we going?' she repeated.

Uncle Ted looked at Nicholas and winked. 'Shall we tell her?' he said in a very conspiratorial manner.

'What's happening?' Sarah said. There was something about her brother, something electric in the air, something that made her own news about Biminy and the kittens suddenly less important.

126

'We're going to Cheltenham,' said her uncle. 'We've just had a very important phone call....'

'I've just had a very important phone call,' Nicholas corrected his uncle, and they both burst out laughing, as if it were the greatest joke in the world.

'Oh for goodness' sake,' protested Sarah, who was beginning to lose patience. 'Who phoned?' she said. But her heart started to pound.

'Guess!'

She shook her head.

'Who do you think?' Nicholas teased, though his eyes had already told her the answer.

'Was it?—Was it . . . ?' she stammered, hardly daring to say the word.

Uncle Ted turned to her, put his hand against her cheek and said softly, 'Yes, love. He just phoned from Cheltenham. He's longing to see you.'

'Daddy,' Sarah whispered. She turned to her brother, but he was a blur of tears. 'Oh Nick,' she cried, 'Daddy's come back at last.'